FLY FISHING THE PACIFIC INSHORE

STRATEGIES FOR ESTUARIES, BAYS, AND BEACHES

FLY FISHING THE PACIFIC INSHORE

STRATEGIES FOR ESTUARIES, BAYS, AND BEACHES

BY KEN HANLEY

Dolph— Don't believe everything he says?! — Shewey

Dolph—
3 cheers to wild adventures and wild fish! It's all about sharing with family and friends (even Shewey!). — Ken

GREYCLIFF PUBLISHING COMPANY
Helena, Montana

Cover design by Geoffrey Wyatt, Helena, Montana
Typeset in Minion and ITC Fenice Light by Geoffrey Wyatt, Helena, Montana
Printed by Color House Graphics, Inc., Grand Rapids, Michigan

10 09 08 07 06 05 04 03 02 01 00   10 9 8 7 6 5 4 3 2 1

Library of Congress Cataloging-in-Publication Data

Hanley, Ken
    Fly fishing the Pacific inshore : strategies for estuaries, bays, and beaches /
by Ken Hanley.
            p. cm.
    Includes bibliographical references (p.).
    ISBN 1-890373-11-7 (alk. paper)
        1. Saltwater fly fishing—Pacific Coast (U.S.) I. Title.

SH464.P3 H36 2000
799.1'6663—dc21   00-057294

For Sierra Rose

CONTENTS

ACKNOWLEDGMENTS

I KNOW YOU'VE HEARD IT BEFORE, but the fact of the matter still remains. Without an extensive network of support, this work couldn't have been completed. I'd like to give special thanks to the following individuals who provided both technical and personal support for this project: Gary LaFontaine, Stan Bradshaw, Hall Kelley, Glenn Kishi, Dan Blanton, Kristen and Jamie Lyle, Jay Murakoshi, Tony Papazian, Mike Trotter, Bill Matthews, Peter Piconi, John Shewey, Bud Bynack, and Geoff Wyatt.

In addition, I'd like to recognize the encouragement and assistance I received from the staff of Baranof Wilderness Lodge and Clayoquot Wilderness Resort.

Over the decades, I've been fortunate to work with terrific students. Sharing in their learning curve has been a thrill and cherished privilege. There's no doubt in my mind, those collective adventures have made me a better person. I've drawn from that pool of experiences for the creation of this book.

FLY FISHING THE PACIFIC INSHORE

STRATEGIES FOR ESTUARIES, BAYS, AND BEACHES

INTRODUCTION

I'VE GROWN UP WITH THE ADAGE "10 percent of the anglers catch 90 percent of the fish." Those might not be the exact figures, but the essence of the observation is correct. I've witnessed time and time again the same people succeeding because they fish with a confidence that is based on solid background information and refined field technique. Luck has very little to do with their success.

Successful anglers employ two kinds of skills. They're keen observers of the natural world, naturalists by inclination, if not by training, and they're competent technicians, able to employ adroitly and refine imaginatively the ways they use the equipment they bring to a sport that takes them to natural scenes they love. These skills complement each other especially well in fly fishing. The gear and techniques of fly fishing require those who use them to understand and appreciate the natural realm. They also require both a deft touch and a keen eye. So does developing an understanding of the natural world, which is the one sure way to become a better fly fisher.

As a fly-fishing instructor, I've seen many trout anglers demonstrate that the skills of a naturalist and the skills of an angler go together. Most trout aficionados can speak at length about insect hatches and river flows. They've often studied the effect of water temperature on fish behavior, and they display an understanding of spawning and breeding cycles, as well. They can identify the characteristic signatures of trout feeding on particular kinds of insects at each stage of the insect's life. It's clear that they've spent time learning about the river's environment and its inhabitants and have applied what they learned to the techniques they bring to freshwater fly fishing. In addition, they have spent countless hours perfecting their technical skills, working on their casting and presentations. They developed both sets of skills by being willing to ask questions, seek answers, and draw inferences. In many domains and in many ways, they were curious and always ready to pay attention to what was going on around them.

Yet when the same anglers approach fly fishing in salt water, they seem to lose sight of the principles that made them good anglers back on the spring creeks and freestone streams. They know the marine tackle is different. Saltwater line designs, rod actions, and fly patterns clearly demand variations in technique. And nothing could be more different than the natural environment of saltwater fly fishing. Yet few will take the time to explore those differences prior to making a trek to the ocean. Without much thought to tides and current, weather patterns, food chains, spawning and breeding variations, habitat details, or gamefish biology, they head for the coast expecting to experience the same degree of success they've come to enjoy in the freshwater kingdom.

Let me be blunt. That ain't gonna happen! If they'd tap into the passion they've developed for understanding the trout's world and direct it to the saltwater world and the techniques of fly fishing appropriate to it, they'd once more stand a chance of joining the 10 percent of anglers who catch 90 percent of the fish. Make no mistake about it, marine environments and the gamefish that inhabit them are highly specialized. The skills needed for gaining success are still the same, however. All you need do is actively engage the world with an inquisitive disposition, employing the same skills that brought success in freshwater angling.

This book is meant to make that process easier—to help bridge the gap between the worlds of freshwater and saltwater angling with a fly. I want to welcome you to the world of inshore fly fishing along the Pacific coast. With this book, I endeavor to introduce anglers to the unique fisheries found along the protected outer coast, the open coast, and in the quiet waters encompassing enclosed bays, sounds, estuaries, and sloughs. I've no doubt that exploring these various angling environments will expand your fly-fishing pleasures.

To facilitate your entry into this world, I've adopted what I refer to as the Trident Curriculum. We'll explore the characteristics of habitat. We'll examine the behavior of a wide variety of specific gamefish. In addition, we'll consider equipment design, selection, and field techniques. Place, inhabitants, and equipment: the three points of the Trident Curriculum should offer you a logical path toward future success in fly fishing the Pacific salt.

Part 1 covers the overall effects of tides and the variety of specific environments found along the Pacific coast, with special reference to estuaries, bays, and beaches. Part 2 examines in detail the principal gamefish to be found there and the tactics that have been developed for pursuing them. Parts 3 and 4 cover the tackle and techniques appropriate to West Coast saltwater fly fishing, the prey species favored by Pacific gamefish, and the fly patterns that imitate them, along with the types of watercraft that can be used in fly fishing the inshore environments of the Pacific. Finally, Part 5 gives tying instructions and fly portraits for the fly patterns mentioned in this book.

As you'll see, fly fishers working both afoot and afloat have ample opportunities to sample the outstanding saltwater fisheries of the West. The species present there allow year-round exploration. Tackle options vary from outfits suitable for any trout stream to 10-weight setups that can stop a tuna. Techniques vary from top-water fishing to ways to send a fly deep into the abyss. The options are many, and the fisheries are diverse. And because saltwater fly fishing along the estuaries, bays, and beaches of the Pacific is still in its infancy, compared with the practices and traditions that have grown up over centuries in freshwater trout fishing, the techniques involved are always in constant evolution. It's an area of angling that rewards asking questions and seeking answers, because there are many questions yet to ask and answers yet to find. Out there, you're really out there. Let's go!

PART 1
HABITAT

To maximize any fly-fishing adventure to the coast, you'll need to understand the influence of tides. There's no other single factor that has such a dramatic daily effect on marine life and its habitat.

The following explanation of what actually creates tides and how tides affect local conditions was provided by Marc Alan Born, of Pacific Publishers, the creator of Tidelog. (See the Bibliography for more information on this resource.)

Sunset along Northern California's coastline.
PHOTOGRAPH BY KEN HANLEY

Earth's tides are produced by the gravitational attractions of the moon and sun. Although the moon is millions of times smaller than the sun, its proximity to the earth gives it a tidal influence more than twice that of the sun. Opposing the direct gravitational forces are centrifugal forces that produce a tidal bulge on the side of the earth away from the moon, resulting in two high tides per day for most locations.

Twice a month, when the moon is full and when it's new, the moon, sun, and earth are more or less aligned. The resulting "spring tides," which get their name from their powerful expansion and contraction, like a spring, have a greater range, with higher highs and lower lows than are ordinarily found the rest of the month. Conversely, when the moon is in a quarter phase, the moon and sun tend to counteract, rather than reinforce each other. The resulting "neap tides," which get their name from an obscure Old English word meaning "without power of advancing," are much weaker. Neap tides occur on alternating weeks between spring tides.

Since the moon's orbit around the earth is elliptical, its distance varies by about 11 percent during a month. At perigee, when the moon is closest to the earth, its tidal influence is increased. The opposite is true at apogee, the farthest point away from the earth in its monthly orbit. Likewise, on an annual, rather than monthly cycle, the sun's influence is increased at perihelion, when the earth is closest to the sun, and decreased at aphelion, when it is farthest away. When a new or full moon's spring tides coincide with perigee, augmented in winter by the sun's position of perihelion, the result is dramatically increased tidal ranges.

The moon's declination also affects the tides. Its orbit is inclined relative to the earth's equator, and the moon appears to cross over the equator twice a month, reaching maximum north declination and maximum south declination about two weeks apart. Either point of maximum declination tends to encourage inequality between a day's two high (or low) tides. This effect is definitely more pronounced along the Pacific coastline.

Those are the basics as expressed by Born. It gets a little more complicated, however. The earth makes a single rotation every twenty-four hours, but the moon orbits at a slightly faster rate. This discrepancy causes a daily fifty-minute lag before any given spot on earth catches up with the moon. In other words, the moon rises fifty minutes later each day. The tide sequences migrate around the clock with it. Approximations are all you really need, though, so it's easy just to figure that the highs and lows will be about an hour later each day. If today's maximum flood took place at 2:00 p.m., you can assume tomorrow's equivalent phase will occur some time around 3:00 p.m.

The U.S. National Oceanic and Atmospheric Association (NOAA) is the organization responsible for providing tidal data in the United States. The National Ocean Survey is a division of NOAA created to collect and analyze this material. The National Ocean Survey has a Pacific Operations Section, located in Seattle, that provides exclusive coverage along the Pacific coast.

NOAA has designated specific sites for which it gives information about tides. The tidal projections it gives are based on a "mean lower low water" level at each site. That designation refers to the standing water depth at the bottom of an average low tide there. This level is also noted as the "datum line," the zero from which the plus signs and minus signs you see on tide tables deviate. Tidal measurements reflect the amount of water that rises above or drops below this standard base. A flooding tide predicted at plus six feet refers to six additional feet beyond the "mean lower low" level. Minus tides are tides that drop below this level. In many cases, the minus tide will leave the bottom exposed without any standing water present at all at the "mean lower low" point.

There is another set of data with plus and minus signs you'll see on some tide charts, as well. NOAA doesn't supply tide information for every inch of coastline, bay, and estuary. Instead, it supplies data in terms of plus and minus time and height corrections with respect to what it calls a "reference station" For example, all of Northern California's tides are predicted using San Francisco Bay as a reference station. The actual site within the bay is located around the Golden Gate Bridge. Tide charts for locations along the outer coastline will usually display a minus sign in front of figures for time and height, because the tide's influence is felt there before the stated prediction inside San Francisco Bay. Locations inland such as large bays, deltas, and so on display a plus sign for these figures, indicating that the tidal effects occur later than at the reference station. It's a simple matter of the flooding tide having to travel farther inland.

In fly-fishing terms what does all this mean? Tides don't affect just water levels, they affect a whole lot of things a saltwater fly fisher needs to consider: access to launch (and take-out) sites, foot access, whether areas where fish hold can or cannot be reached, including optimal depth ranges, plus fly-line selection, optimal time frames for fishing (which also need to be weighed against possible lighting conditions at the time), the extent of flats flooding, the depth of channels and the direction of current flows, gamefish ranges, and accessible forage. Studying tides gives powerful clues as to where you could go, when to be there, how long you'll be there, equipment selection, and what field techniques you might employ.

Information from tide charts also has to be considered together with other relevant data. The actual height of specific tides can be affected by varying weather conditions. Strong winds and barometric swings have the most influence. That means the predictions on the charts are just that—predictions. The tide charts tell you only what would happen if other forces influencing the tides weren't present. So you need to find out about local conditions at the time you plan to fish. The most relevant information about the way tides affect fishing, however, is first-hand local knowledge. If you fish enough, you'll probably build a reliable network of contacts, people who know by experience what to expect. The best way to do that, though, is to become one of those people yourself. Keep a detailed record of your own field excursions. Personal experience plus local knowledge gleaned from others will give you the proper perspective to apply the information you get from tide charts.

It might sound like we've gone from the cosmic regularities of the orbits of the earth and moon down to the uncertainties of tomorrow's weather and the accidents that help determine how the fishing goes from day to day. But cheer up! There are a lot of basic principles that can help you apply what tide charts tell you in order to become a more

effective angler.

Given a choice, try to fish moving water. That means, in general, avoiding the slack water at the bottom and top of tides. Moving water frequently results in more predator/prey encounters. The necessary amount and intensity of flow will vary from one location to the next. It all depends on factors such as the slope of the beach, bottom, or bank, the type of terrain, and the depth and overall size of the area to be affected.

Neap tides are desirable when fishing over reef structure, around kelp beds, along rocky shore habitat, or wading on steep sloping beaches. These tides create a somewhat stable environment to keep both gamefish and prey populations moving in a relatively small area.

Spring tides are desirable for flooding high, shallow terrain. They can provide an exciting temporary fishery at the extreme back reaches of an estuary. Spring tides will be more likely to breach high sandbars at estuary mouths. Anadromous gamefish take advantage of these tides when it comes time for them to migrate into fresh water to spawn.

Flats action is often best during the last two hours of a rising tide and the first two hours of a dropping tide. Predatory fish use the depth of the flooded flats to maximize their coverage of the area in search for prey.

But dropping tides are a perfect time to explore channels, because gamefish often seek the deeper habitat as tides recede. Conversely, channels are the first habitat gamefish must negotiate during the initial flood of an incoming tide.

Spring tides create the strongest currents in compression zones.

Work channels during a dropping tide or first two hours of incoming tide.
PHOTOGRAPH BY GLENN KISHI

These occur wherever the terrain or structure forces the tide through a constricted opening—for example, between two islands. The powerful currents that result concentrate or trap prey populations against jetties, riprap, and other types of cover.

If you encounter conditions that are contrary to what you expected, adapt and take notes. With nature's infinite variations, there always are exceptions to any rule. Don't be afraid to experiment!

Estuaries are influenced dramatically by freshwater flows.
PHOTOGRAPH BY GLENN KISHI

"CALM": I HAVE TO PUT THAT WORD IN QUOTES whenever I speak of the Pacific's estuaries, the lower parts of rivers that empty into the sea, where ocean tides enter, bringing salt water that mixes with fresh water. In relative terms, estuaries are indeed a great deal calmer than the habitat found along the open coast. In estuaries, the harshness of the ocean environment is tempered. At the same time, though, the freshwater world gets a reminder of the ocean's force. Don't make the mistake of interpreting "calm" as suggesting that conditions don't change, though. These protected waters fluctuate in surface area, depth, and salinity, bottom structure, and bottom cover. The result is a hybrid environment in constant change where transient gamefish species have to adapt to short-term conditions. But numerous creatures and plants also claim this habitat as a year-round residence and have developed the ability to endure these same environmental shifts over the long term. So all in all, estuaries offer the fly fisher an amazingly accommodating environment to explore. These waters also provide feeding, breeding, and nursery grounds for a large number of Pacific gamefish and their favorite prey.

Estuaries flow in a wide variety of marine environments, including bays, sounds, and inlets. Though the differences may appear to be merely semantic, they in fact dictate differences in gamefish populations, forage species, bottom structure, plant cover, and the fauna that lives in it. Recognizing these differences is the first step toward a successful fly-fishing adventure.

The overall size, shape, and depth of an estuary depends on topographic features and water flow. The influence of topography produces a wide variety of estuaries, including drowned river valleys such as the Umpqua River estuary, fault-block estuaries such as the San Francisco Bay complex, and deepwater fjords, such as are found in southeast Alaska, British Columbia, and Washington's Puget Sound. Over the course of

Classic deepwater fjord of southeast Alaska.
PHOTOGRAPH BY GLENN KISHI

geologic time, in areas where the sea level rose in relation to the land mass, significant flooding occurred. Typically this meant low-gradient rivers and their valleys were drowned and transformed into estuaries. They became broad, shallow, sweeping habitats likely to have numerous tidal creeks. In this type of estuary, tidal influence can extend quite a distance inland. Where the land mass has risen in relation to the sea, as happened in fault-block estuaries, steeper and stronger river flows produced a shorter, narrow estuarine habitat. Where the sea has flooded deeply carved glacial basins, we also get narrow estuaries, as in the fjords of the north. And even smaller, bar-built habitats, where offshore sandbars have risen above sea level and enclose freshwater inflows to shallow coastal waters, can qualify as estuaries.

Each type of estuary presents its own fishing opportunities, and each type requires different fly-fishing strategies, as we'll see when we come to consider the prongs of the Trident Curriculum dealing with gamefish and techniques. The same goes for another set of differences that distinguish different types of estuaries. These involve the way salt and fresh water mix in them. Some, such as the Columbia River estuary, are river-dominated, while others, such as the estuary at Coos Bay in Oregon, are dominated by the ocean's influence. Whether the river or the ocean dominates, the mixing of fresh and salt water creates different salt-wedged, well-mixed, or partially mixed habitats.

Salt-wedged habitat is created when the flows of a large, strong river meet tides that typically have a small range of movement. The results are a well-defined break between the salty marine layer and fresh water. Because salt water is heavier than fresh, the salty layer acts as a "wedge" moving underneath the freshwater layer on the surface. That wedge of saltier water is likely to travel seaward during low tides and farther up the estuary during high tides. Salt-wedged habitat tends to occur in estuaries with deep contours and a narrow profile, such as fjords.

Well-mixed habitat occurs when the river flow is weaker and the tidal range is greater. The stronger the tide's movement into the estuary, the better the mixing of waters. The energy from the larger tidal swings actually pushes the saltwater layer across the surface at first. The heavier salt water then mixes with the fresh water as it begins to settle toward the bottom. Abrupt layering doesn't exist here. This kind of habitat tends to occur in marine-dominated estuaries that are also fairly shallow and expansive.

Partially mixed estuary habitat is a hybrid classification. It can exhibit the qualities of both salt-wedged and well-mixed habitat. It's generally the result of moderately deep topographical contours, moderate tidal range, and moderate river flows.

Smaller estuaries are affected more by seasonal variations than by daily tidal cycles. During the wet winter months, plenty of runoff and maximum high tides keep the estuary mouths free from extreme sedimentation. In the summer, the reduction of runoff causes a temporary sand barrier to isolate the estuary from tidal influence for months.

Tidal movement has a dramatic affect on the creation of currents inside an estuary, as well. Just as you'd expect in a river, natural or artificial constrictions and barriers in an estuary create stronger currents by forcing the tidal flows through reduced openings. Such constriction zones can occur at an estuary's mouth, along jetty walls, and against meanders in the main channel.

Besides the effects of tides and salinity, an estuary derives much of its personality from the composition of its floor. You'll likely find sand or sandy mud to be the predominant substratum. The lower reaches often mirror the surf-zone conditions of the adjacent open coast. Sandy floors are characteristic of this part of the estuary. The sands are often barren or offer little in the way of vegetative cover. As you travel farther away from the mouth, you increasingly encounter a mixture of sand and mud and a wider variety of plant life with eelgrass beds providing key cover. Eelgrass is highly adaptive and can be found throughout most of an estuary's varying substrata.

Life in and around the sandy flats is based on a food chain that begins with plankton, bivalves, worms, and a few crustaceans. The other ecological niches of the estuary offer by far more diverse and abundant food sources to their inhabitants, but in large part because of tidal action, the creatures of these lower sandy flats are constantly supplied with plankton, the anchor of the food chain. Zooplankton in particular is brought into the lower estuary from nearby shallow coastal waters. The estuary's diverse collection of tiny animals also includes larval and juvenile forms of residents from the estuary itself. Most of the gamefish and baitfish found foraging in the lower reaches are simply following the food resources as dictated by tidal movement.

Eelgrass is a highly productive habitat widespread in estuaries.
PHOTOGRAPH BY GLENN KISHI

Eelgrass and seaweed are stabilizers of sorts in the lower estuary. Their roots help slow down the shifting of the sands. As the substratum changes to a sandy-mud composition, the plants also provide a home, or at least temporary shelter, for a growing variety of animals. The eelgrass begins its profuse growth in the early spring and continues growing throughout the summer. The eelgrass and seaweeds support animals that thrive on the blades, stems, and roots of the plants. Shrimp, crabs, and snails occur in abundance. Fish commonly attach their eggs to the plants. Fry and young gamefish forage among the blades. For mature gamefish, the grass beds therefore are a food factory. Baitfish populations might include sculpins, gobies, blennies, anchovies, herring, and sand lances. You can expect both resident and transient populations of gamefish to be found among the grass. Resident species include sand bass and rockfish. Transient predators include stripers, flatfish, and salmon.

Estuaries also include environments that could be called part-time estuaries. These exhibit all the qualities of an estuary only during winter's storms, when they're temporarily swelled by the extreme flows of swollen rivers. After the storms have subsided and the river level has dropped, these part-time estuaries become sloughs, backwaters ringed

Sloughs are typically shallow and bordered by marshland or mud banks.
PHOTOGRAPH BY GLENN KISHI

by mudflats and marshes. They're typically shallow, most often only a few feet deep and rarely more than twenty. For our purposes, we can consider them saltwater habitat that can be either directly connected to the open ocean or isolated from it by extreme tides. Freshwater influences are minimal here. There's no direct flow from a river or stream. There's no upwelling from underground springs. Rain is pretty much the only fresh water to enter a slough.

Sloughs are vibrant habitats based largely on the abundance of detritus found in the system. Detritus is a byproduct of the decomposition of plant matter. In most marine habitats, plants and tiny phytoplankton are at the bottom of the food chain. In sloughs, detritus serves that function. Plants begin to decompose during the early fall. The minute particles into which they decompose are somewhat soluble. They're coated by bacteria, flagellates, and other organic matter. Filter-feeding animals then thrive on these particles as a food source, and the majority of residents in an estuary are filter feeders. The eelgrass beds and algae are so prolific in sloughs that their decaying matter might be the single largest contribution to creating a healthy estuarine environment there. Shallow water also contributes by allowing maximum penetration of sunlight. Daily tides replenish nutrients in the water column, as well, and the environment is protected from harsh wave activity.

Mud is the slough's substratum and gives the slough its unmistakable personality. This habitat is home to creatures that burrow for a living. The upper links of the food chain include worms, clams, and snails. Crabs and shrimp are two more important links in the chain. Baitfish populations again can include sculpins, gobies, blennies, anchovies, and herring. Many of the gamefish foraging in sloughs probe the muddy bottom and work in extreme shallows if necessary. Species you'll encounter there include leopard sharks, flatfish, and stripers.

Four distinct subhabitats are present in most estuaries: the main channel, sand flats and mudflats, including tidal creeks, salt marshes, and uplands. As fly fishers, we're most concerned with the main channel and

Wading the flats is a terrific way to explore estuary habitat.
PHOTOGRAPH BY GLENN KISHI

Clockwise from upper left:
Jetties are the perfect built habitat for year-round productivity.
PHOTOGRAPH BY GLENN KISHI

Pilings, including super-platforms, provide prime habitat for gamefish.
PHOTOGRAPH BY GLENN KISHI

Peter Piconi fishing the docks around San Diego.
PHOTOGRAPH BY GLENN KISHI

flats. The main channel is typically the deepest habitat. It's generally in contact with the outer sea. Currents are stronger, and the tidal effects are more immediate. The eelgrass beds found there are lush and extensive. Baitfish populations fluctuate, but can be bountiful at times. Larger migratory predators are likely to take advantage of this subhabitat. Gamefish often find the channel to be a favorable site for use as a nursery, too. The flats and their small tidal creeks are most viable as sport fisheries during flooding tides. The higher the tide, the better the potential for fly fishing. The flooding tide expands the foraging grounds for gamefish leaving the deeper channel. The narrow structure of flooding tidal creeks frequently helps to confine prey species, too.

Estuaries contain one more subhabitat worth mentioning: the built environment. Harbors are a classic example, offering jetties, wharves, pilings, floating docks, and other artificial structures that provide ideal conditions for significant colonies of plants and animals to thrive. Many of the species found among the built environment are also members of the intertidal habitat of the outer coastline. You'll find seaweeds such as sea lettuce and sugar wrack, winged kelp, and alaria. Barnacles and mussels are present in abundance in the food chain, as are worms, shrimp, and crabs. Numerous varieties of baitfish take refuge here, followed by the gamefish that regard them as a meal.

IMPORTANT SPECIES IN ESTUARIES (E) AND SLOUGHS (S)

PLANTS	BAITFISH	GAMEFISH (CONTINUED)
Eelgrass (E, S)	Northern anchovy (E)	Sand bass (E)
Sea lettuce (E, S)	Slough anchovy (E, S)	Croaker (E)
	Deepbody anchovy (E)	Lingcod (E)
INVERTEBRATES	Pacific sand lance (E)	Cabezon (E)
Mussels, various clams, and	Pacific herring (E)	Barracuda (E)
cockles (E, S)	Shiner perch (E, S)	Halibut (E)
Ghost shrimp (E, S)	Sculpin (E)	Leopard shark (E, S)
Black-tailed shrimp (E)	Plainfin midshipman (E)	Flounder (E, S)
Coon-stripe shrimp (E)	Squid (E)	Mackerel (E)
Skeleton shrimp (E)		Topsmelt (E)
Grass shrimp (E)	**GAMEFISH**	
Lined shore crab (E, S)	Surfperch (E, S)	
Mud crab (E, S)	Cutthroat trout (E)	
Purple shore crab (E)	Salmon (E)	
Opal worm (E)	Rockfish (E)	
Clam worm (E, S)	Striped bass (E)	
Six-lined nemertean (E, S)	White seabass (E)	

Working the wind seams of Warm Springs Bay, southeast Alaska.
PHOTOGRAPH BY GLENN KISHI

"TRANSITION" IS THE KEY CONCEPT for understanding bay species and habitats. The bay's outer edge is the open ocean, while its inner boundaries are shallow reefs and rocky shores. The West Coast's bays are bodies of water that are somewhat protected from the full force of the ocean by the land that surrounds them, but they're still part of the mighty Pacific, and some, such as Monterey Bay, are significant features of the Pacific Ocean itself. In some, too, the near-shore environment often consists of long stretches of surf zone, so anglers fly-fishing bay waters sometimes will need the skills and information appropriate to beach fishing along the more exposed coastline discussed in the next chapter. Others, such as San Francisco Bay or Humboldt Bay, form major parts of estuary systems, and some of the material we've already covered can be relevant to fishing them, as well. But the principal features of bays from an angling point of view are ones that, as transition zones, they often share with the open coast: rocky shores, reefs, kelp forests, and open water. Each of these provides its own opportunities and challenges to the fly fisher.

Rocky shores are a classic feature of Pacific coast bays. With sheer cliffs, shallow, sloping points, pocket pools, terraces, and even jetty walls,

Rocky shores can offer foot access.
PHOTOGRAPH BY KEN HANLEY

rocky shores offer one of the most complex environments you could ever expect to fish, a habitat that provides prey species and gamefish alike with a maze of swirling subcurrents and ambush stations.

Carpets of rockweed mark the upper intertidal zone.
PHOTOGRAPH BY GLENN KISHI

The intertidal region of rocky shores commonly is subdivided into four habitats: the splash zone, the high-tide zone, the midtide zone, and the low-tide zone, although some researchers prefer to combine the high-tide and midtide zones, creating a three-tiered system. Nature has a way of refusing to be neatly categorized like this, however, so the plants an animals that live in each zone don't always live strictly within their boundaries.

The first habitat, the splash zone, is affected by salt spray. It is most likely to be flooded only by the highest of tides. These extreme tides occur just a few days each month. It's a world of snails, limpets, and periwinkles—rarely a productive zone for fly fishing.

The second habitat, the high-tide zone, is covered, and uncovered twice daily with the rhythm of the tides. This zone extends from the mean high-tide level to the mean level of the highest of two daily lows. Here, seaweed communities begin to establish themselves. Rockweeds and sea palms are prominent plant life in the upper reaches. Sea lettuce,

Mussel beds are a highly productive habitat during high tides.
PHOTOGRAPH BY KEN HANLEY

Facing page top:
Surge channels are terrific during neap tide cycles.
PHOTOGRAPH BY GLENN KISHI

Facing page bottom:
Tide pools and finger reefs can provide easy foot access and great action.
PHOTOGRAPH BY KEN HANLEY

Turkish towel, and Iridaea grow on the lower, seaward side of the zone. The presence of a wide variety of algae provides an environment for snails, worms, crabs, shrimp, and sculpins. The high-tide zone is also where you'll encounter colonies of barnacles and extensive mussel beds. The region is frequented by a variety of transient gamefish, including rockfish, salmon, sand bass, and more. Depending on your target species, you can have quite a productive foray into this niche.

The third habitat, the midtide zone, occurs from approximately the mean higher low-tide level to the mean lower low-tide level. This zone is completely submerged during most flooding tides, but still is exposed by most low tides. Tide pools and surge channels are important aspects of the ecology of this area. Various red algae and feather-boa kelp dominate the plant community. A wider variety of crustaceans and baitfish lives in this zone. The whole food chain is quite varied here, which can be a benefit to anglers. Again, you can expect to find transient gamefish populations, including stripers, salmon, and flatfish, moving through the area in search of abundant prey.

The fourth habitat, the low-tide zone, is by far the most productive area for fly fishing along the rocky shoreline. This is where you'll maxi-

mize your chances of encountering larger gamefish. The low-tide zone is continuously underwater on most days. Occasionally, part of the zone is exposed to air for brief periods during the minus tides of each month. The flora and fauna of the region are able to reap the benefits of a more consistent environment. Surf grass, which grows in the low-tide zone is a key plant for distinguishing this habitat from the midtide zone. The interface between this area and deeper waters is marked by the presence of oarweed and larger kelp. The low-tide zone shares a number of gamefish species with neighboring kelp forests and reefs in deeper water, including white seabass, stripers, and calico bass.

Gamefish depend on the tide's influence for access to these habitats. As opportunistic feeders, most predators will adapt their diet to the location, and in rocky shoreline habitats inside bays, that means they eat crustaceans and worms. So flies that imitate these groceries, in particular, belong in your fly collection for bay fishing.

Scientists refer to any coastal area found between the high-tide and low-tide marks as the littoral region. Just beyond this along the rocky shore lies what's known as the sublittoral zone. Reefs and kelp forests form the basis of the ecology here. This is the domain of numerous resident gamefish: calico bass, rockfish, and surfperch. Transient species such as salmon, seabass, stripers, and sharks are frequently found roaming the neighborhood, as well.

Shallow reefs are scattered all along the Pacific in waters less than eighty feet deep. Most are composed of soft shale. In many locations, harder chert deposits are interlaced with the shale. Shale reefs are characteristically pitted by rock-boring clams. Their activity and the burrowing of clams weakens the rock, which slowly but constantly erodes and changes, especially under the pounding of waves from winter storms.

Because they're fairly shallow, shale reefs receive sunlight that allows red and brown algae to prosper. These coat the reef as deep as twenty feet below the surface. The shale reef environment also is often the host to flourishing kelp forests. The deeper the reef, the less sunlight is able to penetrate the depths and the less diversity there is in plant life. At the lowermost reaches, around eighty feet, kelp is the principal plant—with one exception. Red crustose coralline algae can be found well beyond the shale environment, into the world of granite reefs found hundreds of feet deep.

The reef habitat is generally the home for fish that dwell in crevices and caves. The topography allows the creatures to hide and hunt among

ledges, pinnacles, and rock piles. Some species of gamefish choose to roam just above these rocky features, finding it no problem to target various invertebrates and smaller fish as food.

Once the rock-boring clams of the shallow reefs die, their burrows provide habitats for a large number of creatures, including snails, worms, octopuses, and crabs, for starters. Small fish such as blennies, sculpins, and wrasses forage here, and large predators follow. Rockfish, striped bass, leopard sharks, and lingcod all routinely prowl the reef in search of a meal. Halibut also hunt here, especially where the reef is adjacent to an open, sandy bottom.

Kelp forests can be one of the most accessible and productive habitats for exploring with fly tackle. These magnificent stands of flowing cover host over one hundred different species of fish throughout the year. The gamefish populations change seasonally, and what you find lurking among the kelp also will vary with depth, bottom structure, and the forage that's present. Out of this extraordinary collection of visitors, approximately half are common to the region. Flyrodders will find rockfish, kelp bass, perch, salmon, white seabass, and silversides to be the most abundant species in the kelp forest. Striped bass, barracuda, and

Kelp forests are one of the most productive zones for inshore fly fishers.
PHOTOGRAPH BY GLENN KISHI

halibut lurk along the outer edges of the beds. Since most kelp is anchored on reef structure, you'll find the two habitats share some common gamefish populations.

Although kelp is a huge seaweed, it's actually classified as one of the brown algae. Two major species grow along the Pacific. Bull kelp *(Nereocystis)* is the predominant kelp species from Alaska down to Northern California. From the middle of California to Mexico's Baja Peninsula, the giant perennial kelp *(Macrocystis)* predominates, although both species grow throughout the entire range of coastline.

Bull kelp is a short-lived species. It rarely sustains itself for more than twelve months. The northern beds fluctuate dramatically in size and density from year to year. Giant kelp, on the other hand, can live well beyond five years. This life span provides a much more consistent habitat. This is particularly true where the plant is anchored to hard-rock foundations.

The two major kelp species share common characteristics. They don't have roots, but anchor themselves with a complex of netting known as a holdfast. Unlike land-dwelling plants, which require root systems to penetrate a substratum for nutritional purposes, kelps use their holdfasts only as anchoring points. Another shared feature is the ropelike stem, or stipe. The stipe is a thick-walled stalk with the ability to grow rapidly. Under optimal conditions, its growth rate could be measured in feet, rather than inches, in a single twenty-four-hour period. Given the right amount of sunlight, waterborne nutrients, bottom structure, and protection from waves, a single plant can attain lengths nearing one hundred feet in a season. Giant kelp typically has three to four stipes. Bull kelp has a single stipe for each individual plant.

Both species of kelp have bulbous floats that support long, flat blades. The floats, gas-filled bulbs known as pneumatocysts, which are able to support the plant in the strongest of currents or wave conditions, enable a plant's stipe to be buoyed upward near the surface to maintain contact with the sunlight. The blades furnish a principal site for the process of photosynthesis. With a symmetrical cell distribution, both sides of the blade have equal ability to conduct this process. Even the stipe and holdfast of the giant kelp are capable of conducting photosynthesis, however. Giant kelp has a series of small floats situated along the entire length of each stipe. Individual floats are attached to a single broad blade. Bull kelp has a single large float at the very tip of the stipe. The float is attached to a crown of multiple thin blades.

With all those blades buoyed at the surface, it would appear that the kelp bed is an impenetrable habitat. On the contrary, just under that canopy is a maze that begins to open up and reveal a wondrous territory where currents are slowed and sea creatures abound. The protective kelp forest is a perfect shelter for predator and prey alike.

From the convoluted holdfast to the spread of swaying blades above, each plant hosts numerous animals at every level of the water column. Various schooling baitfish and the offspring of numerous gamefish provide a substantial resource of food for larger predators roaming the surface and middle depths. Bottom-dwelling species find sustenance from a variety of invertebrates, including shrimp, crabs, and worms.

Through the normal cycles of growth and decay, the kelp forest creates a large amount of debris, which is itself a significant ecological resource in this environment. Storm waves and heavy currents tear apart portions of the forest. Some of the material sinks to the forest floor. Yet other debris is suspended and swept away to open water. Often the plant pieces get entangled and amass themselves into large rafts. Anglers refer to these free-drifting rafts as "kelp paddies." These miniature habitats offer a unique opportunity for gamefish in the open ocean to exploit a readily accessible food source because each paddy can trap plankton, harbor shrimp and crabs, shelter schooling baitfish, and act as a temporary nursery for young gamefish. It's always worth your while to explore the immediate vicinity of any kelp paddy you come across. Large gamefish have been known to accompany rafts for great distances.

In addition to the rocky shores, reefs, and kelp beds, bays also hold open water. Sometimes over reefs, at other times over vast tracts of sandy ocean floor, this seemingly undifferentiated environment in fact has soft boundaries that are constantly changing with shifting currents and changes in water temperature, surface turbulence, salinity, dissolved nutrients, and light penetration. Although the open-water environment will certainly change with the seasons, it's the daily and hourly changes in these boundaries that are most important to the saltwater angler in open water. It is a challenge to identify those boundaries on any given day, but as with more permanent structure, boundary areas are places that feeding fish always try to use to their advantage, so it's to an angler's advantage, in turn, to learn to use them as well.

Current lanes and current seams are two of the easier ones to identify. They're usually plainly visible. Abrupt changes in water temperature can be measured with a high degree of certainty. Changes in water color also are often indication of temperature changes near the surface. In

areas where upwelling occurs, the color line is quite dramatic. Upwelling currents raise colder water from the depths. As these nutrient-filled waters reach the surface, they push warmer water aside. The result often creates huge surface slicks that trap debris and concentrate plankton along the inshore side of this temperature wall.

The gamefish of the open-water region are forever on the move. They roam with their food resources if the conditions allow. Zooplankton are a key element in the food chain out here. These are minute animals that at times include the eggs and larvae of crabs, shrimp, worms, fish, sponges, and more. The zooplankton graze on the minute plants known as phytoplankton and on other microscopic organisms, migrating up and down the water column with them as the plants respond to changing conditions of sunlight, temperature, and salinity. Once they find optimal conditions, the phytoplankton and zooplankton communities congregate in a layer, attracting larger creatures, including schooling species such as herring, sardines, and anchovies. These plankton feeders in turn attract salmon, sharks, barracudas, and tuna. Seabass, bonito, and mackerel are keen on the schooling baitfish, as well. So where you're likely to find gamefish feeding can vary from the surface to well below, depending on where light, temperature, turbulence, dissolved nutrients, salinity, and current flows cause the plankton to congregate.

Opalescent squid are another key element of the predator/prey relationships of the open-water environment. These creatures feed primarily on small fish and are themselves fed upon by a variety of larger fish and marine mammals. The squid's presence is a sure indication that something larger lurks nearby. There aren't many gamefish of the Pacific that would pass up the chance for a squid dinner.

Facing page top:
The author points to schooling baitfish working along a current seam.
PHOTOGRAPH BY GLENN KISHI

Facing page bottom:
Foam lines are a soft boundary indicating current paths and food resources.
PHOTOGRAPH BY GLENN KISHI

IMPORTANT SPECIES FOR BAYS, INCLUDING ROCKY SHORES, REEFS, KELP FORESTS, AND OPEN WATERS

PLANTS

ROCKY SHORES
Kelp
Rockweed
Red alga
Surf grass
Sea palm
Feather boa

REEFS
Red alga

KELP FORESTS
Brown seaweed
Bull kelp
Giant kelp
Red seaweed
Turkish towel

INVERTEBRATES

ROCKY SHORES
Mussels
Skeleton shrimp
Tiny shrimp
Rock crab
Purple shore crab
Oregon cancer crab
Red *Lineus* worm
Clam Worm
Six-lined nemertean
Leafy paddle worm

REEFS
Mussels
Barnacles
Dungeness crab
Porcelain crab
Rock crab
Spot prawn
Leafy paddle worm
Clam worm

KELP FORESTS
Kelp crab
Opossum shrimp
Rock crab

OPEN WATERS
Euphausiids
Krill
Pelagic red crab

BAITFISH

ROCKY SHORES
Northern anchovy
Deepbody anchovy
Pacific sand lance
Pacific herring
Shiner perch
Sculpin

REEFS
Northern anchovy
Deepbody anchovy
Pacific sand lance
Pacific herring
Shiner perch
Sculpin

KELP FORESTS
Squid
Northern anchovy
Deepbody anchovy
Pacific sand lance
Pacific herring
Shiner perch

OPEN WATERS
Pacific sardine
Squid
Northern anchovy
Deepbody anchovy
Pacific sand lance
Pacific herring

GAMEFISH

ROCKY SHORES
Surfperch
Cabezon
Lingcod

REEFS
Surfperch
Rockfish
Leopard shark
Salmon
Lingcod

KELP FORESTS
Rockfish
Kelp bass
White seabass
Striped bass

GAMEFISH (continued)

Topsmelt
Jacksmelt

OPEN WATERS
Barracuda
Bonito
Skipjack
Blue shark
Salmon
Sierra
Mackerel
Topsmelt
Jacksmelt

IT'S DIFFICULT TO CONVEY TO YOU what it's like to fish the beaches of the Pacific. Perhaps taking a step back into the world of trout fishing might help. While standing on the bank of a stream, your eyes are often drawn to the opposite bank. Though your intellect knows there's a world beyond that bank, your thoughts seldom can pass beyond the limit of what you can see there. I know that when I'm fishing a freestone stream in a gorge or a spring creek in a meadow cradled in

The Pacific's beaches are a frontier for wild adventures.
PHOTOGRAPH BY GLENN KISHI

the mountains, I'm contained, comfortable, content to explore the compact area between the banks. Often, what I find there is, in the end, what I brought with me, an extension of myself and what I know, however keen the moment of recognition might be. That's one of the reasons I go fishing.

On a beach, there are no limits. There's no "opposite bank" to contain your thoughts, nothing to break the world into a scene you can comfortably take in and inhabit. When my eyes turn toward the Pacific, what I find is not myself, but the world. I'm faced with the vastness of the planet, standing on the edge of a continent at the entrance to a realm as foreign to humans as a new galaxy. It places you. The power and immensity of the sea are humbling, yet I feel energized to be in its presence. Often, what I find there, whether I like it or not, is the way things really are. And that's one of the reasons I go fishing, too.

To do that effectively, though, you need to understand the beach and nearshore environment. On any beach, there are three different, yet somewhat overlapping regions of habitat. The first, from the low-tide line out to sea, is continually submerged and is frequently referred to as the "nearshore level." The second, located in the intertidal range, is called the "swash zone." The third region is the "backshore," located at the upper reaches of the beach. The nearshore and swash zone habitats are what we'll refer to as the surf zone. It's the area most important for anglers.

The surf zone exhibits a few key common denominators. It's always affected by tide and current. It's always a place in flux, changing seasonally, daily, and even hourly. The transformations are both subtle and abrupt, at times tumultuous, even treacherous. It's a place of perpetual drama. Although the surf is teeming with wildlife, most of the sport-fish populations here are generally transient, roaming in and out with the changing tides.

Beaches are categorized by the type and size of materials transported there by waves and current. The materials most likely involved include quartz and volcanic sands, stone, shell bits, pulverized carbonates such as plants and the skeletons of animals, and mud. Take a careful look at the deposits on any single beach. You'll find the combination of materials varies, yet there's always a distinct, dominant material that characterizes the location.

Sandy beaches result from the erosion of mountains and sea cliffs. Tiny mountain fragments composed mostly of quartz and feldspar find their way to the ocean via river flows and estuaries. Sea cliff fragments are directly deposited by wave and wind erosion. The size of the particles ranges from fine-grained to coarse, and the fineness or coarseness of the sand helps dictate the type of inhabitants that characterize a individual beach's wildlife community.

Shingle-style beaches are composed of the largest pebbles and rock particles. Commonly known as "cobblestone" beaches, these are created by the heavy scouring effects associated with steep-sloped shores. Most tiny particles of sand, silt, or mud are immediately transported offshore by a strong ebbing tide, leaving the heavier rocks and pebbles behind.

Beach profiles, their degree of slope, are the result of five interlacing elements: wave intensity and direction, sediment type, sediment transport, and the tide cycle. Breakers are the waves that build and collapse the beach environment. The more violent their action, the greater their eroding effects, eventually pulling sand toward deeper water beyond the visible surf line. In this way, a series of long, sandy ridges running parallel to shore is created every winter as large, powerful waves erode the beach and deposit the sand farther out. The steep beach that results is said to be in "storm profile." Swells, the milder, curling waves of summer, carry the sand that was deposited in these sandbars back toward shore, rebuilding the beach and starting the cycle anew. As the beach regains a wide, shallow slope, it's said to be in "swell profile."

These effects are amplified or muted, depending on all the other factors involved. The West Coast's heavy weather comes out of the north. The more northern the exposure of the beach, the more intense the waves' impact and the more dramatic their effects. And what the waves can do also depends on sediment type and transport. These are directly related to particle size. The bigger the material, the less likely it will travel any great distance offshore. Finally, all the affects that waves can have on the shape of a beach are increased by the effect of heavy spring tides during the new and full moon phases of each month.

The dynamic effects of tides, waves, and currents that produce the constant transformations of Pacific beaches create the conditions to which gamefish and their prey must adapt. That means that once you understand how the dynamics of beaches work, you can use the effects they produce to find fish as they pass into and out of this unsettled, churning environment. Most successful fly fishers begin an outing by observing first and casting second. Just as there are visual keys that allow you to find where fish are likely to be in your favorite trout stream, there are features of the surf that allow you to narrow down where the fish may be in that big, big expanse of sand and foam.

Even more than in other settings, it's important here to look for zones where change occurs: from light to dark, deep to shallow, open water to thick cover, warm to cold, and so on. Fish use these zones, which themselves often are in the process of change, for movement, feeding, and concealment. Predator and prey populations both take advantage of them to conserve energy, find food, and ambush prey or escape from being attacked. As you become more adept at recognizing these important zones, you'll find that you've also become more successful as a salty shoreline fly fisher. The basic keys to identifying zones where change occurs are wave structure and currents, both of which are expressions of the underlying beach topography.

Wave structure is by far the easiest element to observe and probably the most reliable. Essentially, you'll be looking for the changes in wave height. The more radical the change, the greater the relevance in identifying a zone where fish may be found.

As a wave travels over or comes in contact with shallow obstacles such as a sandbar, its energy has to go somewhere, and it goes into a crest that breaks. The closer to the surface the terrain is underneath, the higher the wave's crest. In relatively deeper water such as is found in depressions in the surf zone, conversely, the wave's energy is dissipated, and the wave subsides, leaving calmer water. Everything is relative, so don't ask how high the wave should be. What's important is the difference between frothy, foaming crests and places where the wave begins to disappear. You've just identified a meaningful change in the underlying topography

*The author prepares to
work a trough running
parallel to the shore.*
Photograph by Glenn Kishi

of the beach, a zone of transition from shallow to deeper structure.

Waves traveling over a consistently shallow terrain are likely to have a consistent crest height. If you're looking at a wave that's approximately one to two feet high and it exhibits a constant foam cap for its entire length, this indicates that underneath is probably an extensive sandbar. Another indicator of shallow terrain is the way rafting foam looks on the surface. If the foam raft appears netlike or weblike, spreading over a large area, you can be sure it's an indication of shallow habitat.

Between the sandbars created as the rolling surf transports and recycles sand particles from the sea floor and the shore, the most conspicuous feature you'll notice is commonly referred to as a trough. Running parallel to the shore, it's the deeper, flatter water between the sandbars and the waves that break over them. Troughs are highways for both predator and prey species moving within the surf zone. Most beaches along the Pacific coastline have three to four troughs. In some cases, particularly in Southern California and Baja, you'll encounter locations with only one or two.

Currents are another element easily observed. On the surface, you'll see some areas where foam and flotsam tend to concentrate in a long,

*The smaller foam line
indicates a rip cutting
through a trough.*
PHOTOGRAPH BY KEN HANLEY

narrow corridor, rather than in the weblike networks of the shallows. If
the foam is flowing parallel to the beach, it's moving through a trough.
If the foam is being drawn out to sea, you've identified a significant feature we call a rip. Rips are currents that flow in channels that run
perpendicular to the shore, providing entry and exit lanes for the water
and fish that waves bring in. The trough and rip currents also provide
the fish with suspended food, just like currents in a river or wind seams
on a lake's surface. They're prime places to cast your fly.

   Pockets and cuts are two other important aspects of the underlying
topography of the beach. They're usually found among and between scattered rock formations or the components of artificial habitats such as
pilings. The maze these create reduces the heavy blows of current and tide.
Their softer, swirling back eddies provide protection for smaller species.

   So do pools. Anywhere you see deeper, flatter water, you've identified
a pool where fish can find calmer water as the tides ebb and flow. One of
my favorite techniques for finding existing pools is to watch as a wave
floods the beach. As the water begins to recede, keep an eye on the water-

Maximize your efforts by team fishing along the wall of a pool.
PHOTOGRAPH BY GLENN KISHI

Beach wrack can be a pain, but it can also harbor shrimp, crabs, etc.
PHOTOGRAPH BY GLENN KISHI

line. When the wave has receded and before the next one rolls in, look up or down the beach. You may see an "S" curve. The deeper water occurs where the waterline curves higher onto the beach, because there is less resistance from the bottom there. That's where you'll find a pool. As the line curves back toward the ocean, you'll find shallower habitat. The more prominent the high point of the curve, the larger the angling potential of the pool. The surf scouring against the pool's walls also creates a feeding zone for fish.

Beaches don't appear to have the rich plant and animal diversity of the intertidal rocky shore environment. However, don't be fooled. There's a wide array of resident and transient species associated with the beach community.

The surf zone is a tough place for a large plant to establish itself. With the exception of surf grass, most of the plants in this habitat occur as drift algae, better known as beach wrack. This fundamental resource for food and cover is composed of organic materials washed into the area from adjacent rocky shores, kelp beds, and river mouths. It's the basis of a detritus-dominated food chain. This decaying matter provides much of the nourishment for filter feeders and grazers. They in turn support the prey populations necessary for the larger predators to feed in the surf.

The Pacific mole crab, marine worms, soft-shelled clams, baitfish (herring, sand lances, anchovies, sardines, and smelt are the predominant species) and the fry of gamefish are the foremost items in this food chain. Because of their presence, you're likely to encounter an impressive variety of gamefish within the breakers, from quarter-pound dynamos to multi-pound marauders. You can pursue several types of surfperch, plus salmon, striped bass, and more.

Most of the permanent inhabitants of the surf zone are burrowers. It's the only microhabitat that offers these creatures some sense of security. Burrowing provides protection from constant wave impact and from predation. It also provides somewhat stable conditions in a place where temperature and water levels fluctuate during extreme tidal swings.

The particle size and the space between grains of sand has a direct effect on determining the species of crabs, worms, and the other creatures of the beach that burrow in a particular area of the beach and on the abundance of the creatures that live there. They do so because they help determine the amount of water retained below the sandy surface. Coarse beaches allow the water table to filter downward rapidly. Fine-grained cover holds the water table high for a longer period of time. The finer sand particles and the multitude of smaller spaces between them create a thick, souplike habitat. Burrowing animals find this fine-grained cover easier to negotiate. The porosity and permeability of this microhabitat make it a prime territory for establishing large colonies of prey populations.

Beach inhabitants have adapted their movements to the unique world of the tide's ebb and flow. Colonies of sand crabs and clams use the energy of the surf and the currents that run along the shore to colonize and recolonize prime locations along a beach. They can follow the flooding tide toward higher ground or tumble seaward with receding waters, so that they always are in touch with that soupy sand layer where conditions are optimal. The currents that parallel the beach help redistribute the animals up and down the beach as the composition of the beach changes. This complex dance of tide and current is one reason why prey populations fluctuate seasonally and from year to year.

The Pacific mole crab is a premier food item of the surf zone.
PHOTOGRAPH BY GLENN KISHI

Shells of mole crabs, perfectly designed for tumbling and digging.
PHOTOGRAPH BY GLENN KISHI

The Pacific mole crab is a perfectly evolved organism for this environment. It's not like any other crab you might imagine. The adults are about the size and shape of an olive. The shell is oval, smooth, and offers little resistance against water and sand. The mole crab's legs are short and flat, perfect tools for rapid digging. There's no need for a set of pincers, because the crabs are filter feeders. Their diet consists of plankton and detritus.

Because the mole crab uses the energy of each wave to reposition itself in prime habitat, the crab has access to an extremely wide expanse of beach. Burrowing backward, facing the ocean, the crab anchors itself to intercept suspended food particles in the wash. With only its eyes and featherlike antennae above ground, the crab waits for a receding wave to flush food into its antennae. The trapped items are then transferred to its mouth via scraping appendages.

Mole crab antennae create the shimmer announcing the colony's position.
PHOTOGRAPH BY KEN HANLEY

During the summer, the females carry a roe sac secured to their undersides with a hard, protective cover. After the eggs hatch, the young are carried away by the sea. They become drifters as they proceed to develop through a series of molts. As they grow in size, they seek another sandy shore to transform themselves into adults.

The Pacific mole crab is integral to the food chain in the surf zone. The majority of large predators feed upon them. From roe sac to fully developed adults, these creatures provide sustenance to the great gamefish of the surf.

IMPORTANT SPECIES FOR BEACHES (THE SURF ZONE)

PLANTS	BAITFISH	GAMEFISH (continued)
Surf grass	Pacific sardine	Topsmelt
	Northern anchovy	Jacksmelt
INVERTEBRATES	Pacific sand lance	
Various clams		
Ghost shrimp	GAMEFISH	
Opossum shrimp	Surfperch	
Crago shrimp	Salmon	
Pacific mole crab	Striped bass	
Red *Lineus* worm	Halibut	
Two-gilled blood	Leopard shark	
worm	Croaker	

ARE YOU LOOKING FOR A TRUE light-tackle saltwater experience? You'd be hard pressed to find a better group of species to target than the Pacific mackerel, jacksmelt, and topsmelt. This crew adds up to pure, unadulterated fun! They're the perfect quarry for trout-sized tackle and presentations near the surface, where they'll come readily to small streamers. This threesome can provide the bridge between freshwater and briny pursuits. You'll find these sleek gamefish roaming around harbors and estuaries or darting about the edges of kelp beds and cruising the currents of open bay waters. That means they're best pursued from a boat. However, wading flats that have an edge that drops off to deep water can provide fun action, and fishing from jetties can get you into these fish, too.

Pacific mackerel are tough little speedsters.
PHOTOGRAPH BY GLENN KISHI

Ed Berg and I have partnered on fly-fishing adventures as diverse as chasing sea trout and cod in Denmark and wading for surfperch in Southern California. If you want to see two grown men immediately disintegrate into ten-year-olds, put us smack dab in the middle of an all-out "mac attack." The excitement brought on by ravaging mackerel never fails to entertain us—and our own barely controlled lunacy never fails to entertain onlookers. We love those midget missiles!

Pacific mackerel (*Scomber japonicus*) could be considered miniature versions of the larger tuna. They in fact share the same family. The mackerel's body is elongated, sporting a set of fins similar to the tuna's. Small-surfaced fins, twin dorsals, a row of finlets above and below the wrist of the tail, and a forked tail are all classic features of this family. The Pacific mackerel is perfectly designed for a high-speed lifestyle.

Mackerel are a handsome gamefish. Their backs are often a dark green or a blending of dark blue and green. Their most celebrated markings are the black accents found along the back, a series of approximately thirty wavy oblique bars from head to tail. Their sides are a metallic gray that quickly fades into silver near the belly. Another striking feature is the mackerel's radiant red-orange eye.

"Pac macs" are typically fourteen to twenty inches in length. There have been specimens caught up to twenty-five inches, but that was an extraordinary fish. Most weigh from one to three pounds, with plenty of larger fish sprinkled in the mix. The largest of the species is recorded at over six pounds, a true monster of a mackerel.

The Pacific mackerel's range extends from Alaska to Mexico. The largest concentrations occur in Californian and Mexican waters. (Anglers farther north may know this species as the chub mackerel). They tend to frequent kelp forests, tapering points, rocky shorelines, jetties, and channels. In any harbor with a bait barge, an on-the-water live-bait emporium, you'll find Pacific mackerel nearby, hoping to scarf up an easy meal. They begin spawning in late winter, with the peak spawning activity coming around March, April, and May. Mackerel will often travel in huge schools, particularly during the spawn.

These speedsters eat a wide variety of items in their yearly diet. Opportunistic hunters, like all predatory fish, they dine on a mix of larval, juvenile, and small fish species, plus a healthy dose of various crustaceans. Schooling mackerel present a ravenous threat to any prey populations encountered throughout the year. Larger mackerel have been known to eat young squid when squid are easily available.

Tackle choices can begin with 5-weight and 6-weight outfits. You won't need hefty gear, and you could enjoy fishing for Pac macs with your favorite trout stick. However, rod designers are continually reevaluating their saltwater offerings and have become aware that people are fishing lighter-weight rods in the salt. The 6-weights they are coming up with are a perfect match for this game. Among their many attributes, these new rods offer faster action and larger guides to handle saltwater wind conditions and specialty lines. Their tapers also provide power from the butt section. It's nice to have a little extra insurance, since you never know what could be nearby, targeting the mackerel.

Even though Pacific mackerel often seem to be feeding on the surface, a much higher percentage of their predation takes place between five to twenty feet below. You should be prepared to present your fly on a sinking line. I use the kind that consists of an integrated shooting head and running line. I prefer heads with a weight of 200 to 250 grains. My leader has a short, stout butt section of 20-pound test material, then an untapered tippet rated at 10 or 12 pounds. The combined length is generally less than 7 feet.

A fly collection composed of small baitfish imitations, around two to three inches in length, would be ideal. Clouser Minnows, ALFs, Pearl Yetis, and Deep Candy Bendbacks are key patterns in my adventures.

Hooks in sizes 2 and 1/0 do the job nicely.

If you're blind casting, be sure to let your fly sink before beginning your retrieve. If there's no visible feeding activity near the surface, you'll need to entice the mackerel up from below. But try to avoid blind casting—it's generally a low-percentage game. Make an effort to find the natural indicators that will tell you feeding fish may be present: "nervous" surface water agitated by their activity, or feeding birds, or escaping baitfish. Or use a fish finder to locate schools of bait. The electronic aid is well worth the extra expense, but just investing the time to find a feeding school of Pac macs is well worth it.

If you're casting into a ball of skipping bait, try to target the outside edge of the school. Make your streamer break off from the pack as if it were an injured baitfish. Use an erratic tempo in your retrieve, but keep the offering moving. Predators key on injured prey, and there's no marine prey suicidal enough to come to a full stop, especially while in flight from danger. It's now or never for all parties involved.

Instead of going looking for mackerel, you can make them come to you by establishing a steady chum line. You can buy commercial chum or make your own concoction. Either way, the basic "mash" should incorporate bits of anchovies, sardines, and perhaps some shrimp. There's definitely a protocol to follow if you're to develop a highly productive line. Start by targeting an area from the stern of your boat to a few hundred yards down-current. You want to tempt the schooling mackerel to feed up-current, moving toward your cast and presentation. The critical thing is to offer an even dispersal of bait. Once you see evidence of mackerel entering the chum line, tossing out some live bait will trigger their feeding instincts and bring the mackerel into close proximity to the boat. Pinhead anchovies are the preferred choice. An overabundance of bait, though, can quickly ruin the experience. You want to feed the macs your fly, after all, not just feed the macs.

When a Pacific mackerel strikes, strip strike back and hold on. A strip strike sets the hook with a hard strip using your line hand, the tip pointed at the water, rather than by raising the rod tip. Pacific mackerel have a fairly hard mouth and it takes a deliberate, quick set from you to hook one. Once they're hooked, these torpedo-shaped runners can raise a real ruckus. They may appear small by oceanic standards, but the mighty mackerel will show light-tackle flyrodders their backing in no time. Pac macs are becoming stars in West Coast saltwater fly-fishing circles, deservedly so.

Bill Matthews using pin-head anchovies to hype the mackerel bite.

PHOTOGRAPH BY GLENN KISHI

Two additional mighty mites you're sure to find entertaining are the topsmelt (*Atherinops affinis*) and jacksmelt (*Atherinopsis califoriensis*). Names aside, these gamefish aren't true smelt at all. They belong to the fish family known as silversides, which is found worldwide in tropical and temperate seas and which includes the grunion. Topsmelt and jacksmelt are extremely close in appearance, with only minor variations on the position of the anal fin and overall body size. On the topsmelt, the anal fin begins in line with the first dorsal. The jacksmelt's anal fin begins behind it. They share elongated twin dorsals, the lead fin being the smaller of the set. The tail fin is forked and the pectoral fins are fairly pointed. Both species are a bluish green across the back. Their sides sport a distinctly bright silver lateral band over a metallic silver-gray background. Their eyes and mouths are quite small.

Topsmelt have a wide range, from Vancouver Island down into the Gulf of California. Jacksmelt are more prone to travel the waters of Oregon, California, and the Pacific side of the Baja Peninsula. Both species are common inshore inhabitants, favoring bays, kelp beds, and rocky shorelines. They prefer to travel in schools near the surface or in shallow waters no deeper than fifty feet. Sometimes the schools can be quite massive. These silversides spawn during late fall and throughout the winter. They seek sheltered environments because they lay their eggs on seaweed.

Topsmelt have been recorded at slightly over fourteen inches. The Jacksmelt is the larger of the two species, with a broader chest and lengths reported up to twenty-two inches, although they are more commonly found under eighteen inches. The two silversides can vary in weight from half a pound to over one pound. Two-pound jacksmelt are rare, but they do exist.

For these fish, 5-weight outfits are just the thing. I started out fishing for topsmelt and jacksmelt with a standard ten-foot sink-tip line. As the fly-fishing industry developed more sophisticated lines, two lines in particular have become key to my success: an intermediate sinking line and a shooting head weighing approximately 140 grains that I use for deeper presentations. My target zone is usually within the top ten feet of the water column. I work with tapered leaders that have a tippet section rated at 8 pounds. Leader lengths of 7 to 9 feet are practical choices.

Crustaceans are the main source of sustenance for these gamefish. Larval, juvenile, and adult stages are all consumed. It's wise to have your pattern selection on the small side, size 4, 6, 8, and 10. I use CDC Shrimp, Diamond Shrimp, and even assorted bonefish patterns such as Charlies.

Unlike Pacific mackerel, silversides have small soft mouths. Use a soft hand to set the hook. The slip-strike method is an excellent way to protect against overstriking. As you lift the rod tip to set the hook, let a few inches of line slip through the fingers on your line hand. This slack takes some of the force out of the strike, yet still sets the hook without ripping it out of the mouth of these fish. The direct method of simply continuing with a normal retrieve also can be an effective way to set the hook. The key is to execute a soft, but positive strike. It's best to play the fish on the tip of your rod, as well, where there's an inherent cushion to any heavy-handed or sudden, unexpected movements.

Wading anglers can enjoy some terrific silversides action working along the lower sections of most estuaries. River mouths and the lower drainages provide highways for the fish to travel with the tides. Look for rocky points, cliffs, kelp beds, and tapering sandbars.

The surf zone is another viable habitat for wading anglers seeking silversides. Check with local bait shops to find out where the established "smelt runs" occur. Look for calm, protected beaches with low rollers and consistent surf conditions. Remember that these fish aren't bottom feeders. Your tackle and presentations need to work in the upper part of the water column. I frequently present my streamers on a dropper rig. The point fly is slightly heavier and larger than the dropper pattern. The two-fly set allows me to cover the upper part of the water column in a rapid, efficient manner.

My trusty canoe has been the vehicle of choice for my jacksmelt forays, however. It's the perfect craft for accessing quiet back bays and harbors. Anglers with skiffs who choose to venture beyond the confines of an estuary would do well to explore the outer kelp beds. These lush forests harbor plenty of hungry silversides. You can target the numerous open pockets within the kelp. Working individual pockets is known as "pot holing." The technique requires dropping the fly into a pocket and getting it to sink to the proper depth using a short cast and more or less vertical presentation. You can add depth to the presentation by simply adding slack line into the pocket. If you can't handle the tight quarters, concentrate your efforts along the outer edges. You also could always use chum to lure the fish into open waters, if you prefer.

THE MINUS TIDE REVEALED a massive sandbar. For the first time in months, we could gain access to the outside breaker, standing in thigh-deep shallows and yet casting out to the cruising predators in Big Blue. Jay Murakoshi and I were conducting another surfperch clinic in ideal conditions for instructors and students alike: calm waters, low rollers, overcast skies, and a windless dawn.

The sunrise seemed slow in coming, but the creatures of the surf were already at full throttle. Surf scoters were picking off tumbling sand crabs. Brown pelicans were deftly slipstreaming in the troughs of incoming surf. And Brandt's cormorants were feasting among the hordes of silvery baitfish. Dolphins were off in the distance, presumably working over similar forage. These were signs we were in the right place at the right time. Little did we know that all hell was about to break loose and that we were in for a heart-thumping lesson in what can happen when you're fishing the Pacific.

Greg Pedemonte with a prize barred surfperch.
PHOTOGRAPH BY KEN HANLEY

A bait ball of anchovies was clearly visible at the base of a wave. As the wave collapsed in an explosion of silver, baitfish rained about us. The place sparkled with scales and flashes of brilliance, and the surf was lit up like a Fourth of July celebration. A pod of porpoises was in hot pursuit of the anchovies. Not more than twenty feet in front of us were feeding machines weighing over two hundred pounds. We had to honor the wildness. Fly fishing the surf zone never ceases to be an adventure, but this was something else. As I said, out there, you're really out there.

The surfperch we were seeking that day are the gamefish species that a flyrodder can most reliably expect to find in the surf zone. From the frigid waters of Alaska to the sun-drenched beaches of Baja, you can find them just about anywhere.

The Pacific coastline plays host to eighteen different species of surfperch. They range in size from six to eighteen inches and can top the scales at over four pounds. The six most common species are barred surf-

The author and Jay Murakoshi discussing strategies.
PHOTOGRAPH BY GLENN KISHI

Redtail surperch are the dominant species of the northern coast.
PHOTOGRAPH BY KEN HANLEY

perch (*Amphistichus argenteus*), calico surfperch (*Amphistichus koelzi*), redtail surfperch (*Amphistichus rhodoterus*), walleye surfperch (*Hyperprosopon argenteum*), silver surfperch (*Hyperprosopon ellipticum*), and shiner surfperch (*Cymatogaster aggregata*).

Surfperch are handsome gamefish. Their bodies are compressed and elliptical, and their colors are brilliant: silvery blue and brassy olive dominate. Vertical barring, horizontal stripes, and multicolor flecking are striking accents. The husky barred and redtail surfperch dominate the surf zone. Redtails (also referred to as pinkfins) are the kings of the northern realm. The barred surfperch takes top honors from the San Francisco Bay Area's coastline southward to the rugged frontier of Baja's central coast.

The protected environments of inner bays, estuaries, and tide pools harbor a different group of surfperch: pile surfperch (*Damalichthys vacca*), rubberlip surfperch (*Rhacochilus toxotes*), striped surfperch (*Embiotoca lateralis*), rainbow surfperch (*Hypsurus caryi*), and white surfperch (*Phanerodon furcatus*). Their coloration is typically darker than that of the sandy-beach species, with mottled or striped accents. The

basic background colors range from variations of black to brown, although muted gray-silver and olive also are common. Two species are covered with brilliant blue and orange stripes or vertical bars. Peak season for these species is the spring and summer months. Concentrate your efforts around both built and natural cover. Docks, pilings, rocks, even grass beds and various seaweed forests harbor these beautiful gamefish.

The best time to find surfperch along the sandy beaches of the Pacific depends on two factors: the breeding cycle of the fish and the conditions of the surf itself. Depending on where you're located, the first significant period of the breeding cycle extends from November well into February. This is when perch enter the surf zone to mate. From late autumn through the early winter months, you'll find your catch is dominated by males loaded with milt.

The gestation period for perch is approximately five months, and from May through July you'll find the females back in the breakers completing the spawning cycle by releasing their young. Surfperch are viviparous, and these "live bearers" usually seek the calmer pools or deeper troughs to give birth. It's quite easy to identify a "ripe" female. You'll see a protrusion resembling a small golf ball near the anal fin. Don't handle the adult too long. It could cause undue stress, resulting in the female dropping her young early. A typical litter can be from three to ten fish, with the average around six, although barred surfperch can bear from four to over one hundred young, with the average around thirty. Newborn perch young are between 1½ and 1¾ inches long.

But you won't always find surfperch along the beach, even during these two seasons. If heavy surf makes the shoreline habitat too rough for feeding, mating, and giving birth, the fish favor far deeper haunts. Redtails routinely can retreat to depths of more than 100 feet, and barred surfperch are comfortable at over 200 feet. Shiners can lurk at 400 feet and more. That's why there are going to be days when you can't even buy a fish in the surf zone.

Even under the conditions that surfperch favor, the surf zone is a tumultuous place in which to have to survive. However, nature has a wonderful way of providing species with the tools needed to do so. Take the surfperch's mouth structure, for example. It's perfectly adapted for finding and capturing prey in the turbulent world of the surf zone. The mouth works much like a vacuum's hose, extending into a cone to enhance the suction needed to draw in food items. Debris and food are turned and churned in the sandy wash of the surf, and the perch has little time to distinguish items by sight, so its primary feeding technique is "oral winnowing." Feeding near the bottom, it simply vacuums in whatever comes its way, rolls the stuff around in its mouth, and discards anything that isn't considered acceptable food. Acceptable food consists of crustaceans, clams, marine worms, and to a lesser degree, tiny fish.

Take a close look at the throat of a perch, though, and you'll find a clue to its principal food source. Located deep in the throat is a fully developed set of teeth. These are blunt, but they're substantial crushing tools. The perch are built to favor sand crabs and shrimp in their diet.

As a consequence of the way they feed, perch frequenting the surf also can employ what's commonly known as "random feeding behavior." If the fish bumps into something by chance, it will try to sample it as a food item. Opportunistic feeding is critical to the survival of these gamefish. In the surf zone, fish can't afford to be hypercritical, and while it doesn't hurt to try to "match the hatch," surfperch are at the other end of the scale from finicky rising trout. Get something foodlike in front of them, and you're in business.

To ply the Pacific surf zone, I recommend outfits rated at 7-weight or heavier. Even though the fish are relatively small, and even though you usually won't need to cast much more than thirty to forty-five feet, you need to match your tackle to the rigors of the habitat, not to the size of the target species or the distances involved. Heavy hydraulics, onshore winds, weighted flies to get the presentation to the fish, and an unstable casting platform will put extreme pressure on your equipment, and you need something heavy enough to stand up to the challenge.

Because the perching game requires constant casting, though, 10-weights are probably as heavy as you should go. Working with lighter rods can be a real blessing in most surf-zone situations. I know plenty of Southern California anglers who enjoy using 6-weight outfits under extremely calm conditions. However, if you plan on pursuing larger gamefish such as halibut or flounders, stripers, or even roosterfish down in Baja, you'll want the option of increased leveraging that 9-weights and 10-weights will provide.

Line selection is pretty simple for surfperching. Use any line that gets your fly down quickly to these bottom feeders. Over the decades, I've worked successfully with 13-foot sink tips, standard shooting heads, and specialty lines with integrated shooting heads and running lines. I would recommend that you avoid full-sinking lines, though. They sometimes won't allow you to cast, let the fly sink, retrieve, pick up, and cast again as

Grinding teeth deep within the throat help trap prey, especially crustaceans.
PHOTOGRAPH BY KEN HANLEY

fast as you need to before the next wave pounds you and your tackle. From central California into the Pacific Northwest, the heavy surf makes this a challenge throughout the year.

Among shooting-head systems, most West Coast anglers prefer heads rated from Type 4 to Type 6. The same sink rates apply for sink-tip designs. With integrated shooting heads and running lines such as the

Teeny TS Series or the Rio Deep Sea lines, I find the lines rated at or a little over 200 grains handle most of my needs. During the winter, with its heavier surf, I prefer to use lines rated at 300 or 400 grains.

Because the surf zone is such a turbulent environment, I look for ways to increase my control from rod to fly. Limiting the length of my terminal system helps accomplish that. Generally, I work with a leader that's a straight piece of mono rated at 10 pounds. Starting at low tide, I use approximately 6 feet of leader material. As the tide builds, I chop the system back, usually ending the day with a leader about 3 or 4 feet in length.

Keep in mind that you want to draw attention to your fly in a turbulent environment awash with debris. Your retrieve is what accomplishes this. I find that longer pulls of one to two feet help to create a desirable animation that fish can key on and that distinguish my fly from the inanimate objects tumbling in the surf zone. I also prefer not to use an erratic tempo in my retrieve. The surf itself provides plenty of that action. Consistency in the length of your pulls and the tempo of your retrieve also will provide you with a higher degree of contact with your fly.

Part of the challenge of surfperching is to locate feeding perch and present them with something that, at that time and place, looks to them like a possible food item. To do that, for the past few years, Jay Murakoshi and I have preferred a two-fly rig based on a combination of flies that gives the perch a choice of sand crab and shrimp patterns. Our dropper is most often a small, unweighted shrimp imitation. The point or lead fly can either resemble a crab or its colorful roe sac.

A great collection of fly patterns for surfperchin' safaris would include the following: the Surfpercher Red, Jay's Micro Shrimp, Jay's Grass Shrimp, my Surf Grub, a Rusty Squirrel Clouser, and a Near 'Nuff Sculpin. The best hook sizes are 2 and 4. Weighted Woolly Buggers and shad flies are also commonly used.

Remember that as opportunistic feeders moving into and out of the surf zone, perch are constantly on the move. That means you need to be, too. Don't stay in one place too long, or you'll lose the ability to work the tide. Usually all it takes is fewer than a dozen casts to find out if there are any perch interested in your fly. Don't try to stake a claim to beachfront property. Instead, force yourself to cover the beach and you'll likely jump a school that can provide fast action.

IT WAS ONE OF THOSE SITUATIONS. Your buddy is yelling and you just can't hear him. Though we were only fifteen to twenty feet apart, I still didn't understand what all the commotion was all about. Dan Blanton was playing a rockfish to the boat's stern, while I was standing on the bow, concentrating on retrieving my fly. The boat had rotated a bit, repositioning itself during the drift, and I couldn't see the retrieve path of my streamer. Apparently it had swung close to my partner's fish.

The author with a beautiful dusky rockfish.
PHOTOGRAPH BY GLENN KISHI

Dan had lured his prize out from a small shelf crowned with kelp. As the quillback came closer to the boat, Dan became more animated. His fish had drawn the curiosity of another predator. A much larger game-fish. A gamefish with hundreds of teeth.

Dan was yelling, "Kenny, strip! Strip! Strip! There's a ling shadowing your fly!" Apparently when my minnow imitation had swung into sight, this mouth with fins became interested in my streamer. I couldn't see a thing, although Dan was staring right at the fish. At first, I thought he was playing a practical joke, and I didn't bother to alter my retrieve. My partner couldn't believe I didn't believe!

It was easy to see Dan was getting flabbergasted, so I began to move the minnow at a faster clip. Directly between us, not more than a few feet from the skiff, a beautiful mottled lingcod devoured the fly. It was the perfect take—in full view of two perfectly excitable guys. If I hadn't experienced yet another of my characteristic brain locks during the final moments of landing this beauty, you'd have a tremendous photo to go with this tale. Still, that adventure was pure magic.

The West Coast's many marine environments are home to huge schools of rockfish, the *Sebastes* clan. A wide variety of species can be found in habitat ranging from the intertidal zone to deepwater reefs. Rocky shores providing holes, crevices, shelves, and terraces are prime environments. Inshore pinnacles and sea stacks are always a good bet. In a few cases, kelp and eelgrass beds also will house these predators. There are sixty-eight species of rockfish in the genus *Sebastes* in Pacific coastal waters. Two species in the genus *Sebastolobus* also make their home along the coastline. At least a dozen different species are on tap for the inshore angler. Fly fishers will find black rockfish (*Sebastes melanops*), blue rockfish (*Sebastes mystinus*), olive rockfish (*Sebastes serranoides*), yellowtail rockfish (*Sebastes flavidus*), dusky rockfish (*Sebastes ciliatus*), and widow rockfish (*Sebastes entomelas*) most commonly enticed to their offerings. Vermilion rockfish (*Sebastes miniatus*), copper rockfish (*Sebastes caurinus*), quillback rockfish (*Sebastes maliger*), Grass rockfish (*Sebastes rastrelliger*), and black-and-yellow rockfish (*Sebastes chrysomelas*) are available, too.

These are nonmigratory fish. Local populations will occupy a relatively small geographic range, staying close to their natal habitat.

Sebastes are a robust lot, with thick, chunky bodies, rather than the long, slender shapes of open-water, surface-oriented species. A rockfish is built much like a largemouth bass. They sport thick shoulders, a short wrist at the tail, and fins with a large surface area, affording explosive movement. Their pectoral, pelvic, and anal fins are leatherlike, a perfect adaptation for crawling through abrasive cover.

Most of the adults are around two feet in length. Some species can attain lengths of three feet or more. Shallow-water rockfish weigh from one to six pounds. Deep-water specimens commonly push the scales well past the ten-pound range.

The eyes of these fish are quite large, considering the surface area of the rockfish's head. This indicates, in part, that the species does well in low-light environments. Their eyes are also located in a high forward position that helps them see in tight cover, where they can bury themselves, leaving only their eyes exposed, and in structure that otherwise would limit their viewing area.

Although you will frequently run into fish working schooling bait in open water, rockfish feed primarily on smaller fish and crustaceans, ambushing them in the cover where they lurk. Schooling *Sebastes* will target krill, anchovies, herring, sand lances, and sardines. Bottom-hugging species zero in on shrimp, crab, sculpins, and other rockfish. It's quite a menu for the fly fisher to imitate. Once you account for the common characteristics in this food chain, however, you'll be pleased to find that you can work with a relatively small selection of fly patterns. Hook sizes will vary from 2 to 3/0. On rare occasions, you might find need for patterns in size 4 or 6.

When it comes to saltwater fly patterns, the first thing I think of is baitfish. In Pacific waters, there are at least six different species you can count on to draw the attention of most predators in the nearshore or inshore environments. Sardines, herring, anchovies, lanternfish, smelt, sand lances, and gamefish fry are daily choices on the food-chain menu. These fish generally range from two to ten inches in length. Most are typically narrow and elongated, with immature gamefish exceptions to this rule.

To match these baitfish, concentrate on patterns with either blue or green backs and silver or white below. The most productive sizes for rockfish can range from two to five inches in length. Salty predators are a tough, wild bunch. You'll need a hearty fly to stand up to their aggressive behavior. Deceivers, ALFs, and Sea Habit Bucktails are terrific choices for this application. I'd also recommend carrying some balsa or foam poppers of your choice. There are plenty of opportunities to cast to surface-busting rockfish.

Rockfish also feed on sculpins and other bottom-oriented baitfish. Flies to imitate these should be on the darker side. Orange, olive, brown, and black are good choices. The flies should be short, but bulky. Robust patterns can be dynamite because they push water, alerting rockfish to their presence. A Tropical Punch would be a classic choice here. The Gold Buccaneer is a trusty tempter and accounts for much of my catch. Another very effective pattern is a simple Rabbit-Strip Fly (aka Bunny Leech, Tarpon Bunny, etc.).

You can dial right into the crustacean bite with my Labyrinth Crab, Clouser Minnows, and any pattern imitating grass shrimp. If you're casting a fly at night, you might find the rockfish have keyed on clouds of crab larvae and krill. These tiny morsels are best represented with sparse ties such as the Crazy Charlie, the crystal pink version.

Rods and lines for rockfish are straightforward. You just need to be prepared to handle the unexpected. After all, we are talking about throwing a fly into the Pacific, aren't we? I believe a 9-weight outfit is ideal for this fishing. Want to go lighter? Sure you can . . . just remember that any rod you choose needs to have backbone. There will be numerous occasions when you'll be required to lift or leverage with the rod.

The typical line in use for rockfish is a shooting-head system, but any sinking line will get your fly deep, and getting your fly down deep is usually more important here than making long casts. Personally, I prefer the lead-core shooting head commonly known as LC-13, which weighs 13 grains to the foot, or an integrated shooting head and running line rated at 450 grains. You're more likely to be effective with forty feet of line under your boat than with forty feet of line planing on the surface

*Use caution when han-
dling rockfish to avoid
venomous spines.*
PHOTOGRAPH BY GLENN KISHI

behind the craft. Presentations, however, can range in depth from more
than sixty feet to just under the surface. A major strike zone occurs at
around fifteen to twenty feet along most of the Pacific coastline. But
because there are times when surface presentations are indeed called for,
I round out my tackle with an intermediate line for working poppers or
sliders.

Leaders and tippets should be short and stout. Often the entire system is 6 feet or less. A butt section of 20-pound to 25-pound test coupled
to a tippet of 10-pound or 12-pound test is highly effective here. I prefer
a light tippet in case I get trapped and wrapped. I want to be able to sac-
rifice the terminal tackle in order to save my rod and fly line from any
damage.

If you need to handle rockfish, please show extra caution. Rockfish
are in the same family as scorpionfish, and most rockfish species have
slightly venomous spines located in their dorsal and anal fins. Reactions
from the toxins are generally pretty mild irritations. However, if you've
experienced severe allergic reactions to other toxins, you could be subject
to the same with rockfish venom. Poisons aside, the spines can still produce painful damage if you're haphazard with your handling technique.

August and September provide fly fishers with the calmest seas of the year, and these also are the months of the prespawn migration of rockfish into shallower waters. This provides anglers with access of skiffs the best opportunity to target these species. Like surfperch, most rockfish species are viviparous. Insemination occurs during the late summer. In the autumn, these gamefish begin to congregate in nearshore waters to prepare to spawn. The females spawn beginning in January. Then, in the spring and early summer, they drop down into deeper haunts again.

Sebastes are very slow-growing fish. A twelve-inch black rockfish is four to five years old, and a twelve-inch blue is six to nine. In many species, the growth rate also slows down in older fish. The Alaska Department of Fish and Game has determined the age of sample rockfish from California's Farallon Islands with these results: a yelloweye rockfish (*Sebastes ruberrimus*) just over two feet long was sixty-five years old, and a specimen of just under twenty-seven inches was seventy-three. And breeding maturity isn't attained until most species are at a minimum of twelve inches long. Rockfish are a fragile resource, and our rockfish populations are natural treasures requiring more informed management to insure their future health. Don't assume that catch-and-release fly fishing is limited to blue-ribbon wild-trout fisheries.

Adult rockfish found in the more northerly latitudes of the Pacific coast frequent shallower water. Exploring the Pacific Northwest's kelp beds and smaller coves can bring explosive top-water fly-fishing action. The structure, cover, and tide cycles of the region promote such top-water feeding behavior. I can remember days when feeding rockfish have churned the surface into a froth. The edges of entire kelp beds stretching hundreds of yards were inundated with school after school of erupting prey and crashing predators. It's a common occurrence in these cold-water regions.

Have you ever thought of rockfishing from a jetty or a dock complex at night? It can be the answer for anyone looking for *Sebastes* feeding on the surface. Fly fishers afoot can experience some fantastic action during this time by capitalizing on the change that darkness makes in the rockfish's environment. There's little or no mirror effect on the surface to mask their prey against a shining, glassy background. For a predatory species like the rockfish, equipped with those large eyes, it becomes as easy to see topside as it does in the inky depths, and at night, it becomes as productive for them to feed near the surface as it would be to feast on

Another great night session comes to a close at sunrise.
Photograph by John Shewey

the bottom.

We can even draw the rockfish up to the surface. Using a few well-positioned lanterns will entice their prey to the wide variety of items in the food chain that react to the beacon, and the rockfish will follow, much like crappies attracted to bugs flocking to a light set by an angler on a favorite lake. And you may attract more than rockfish. The smorgasbord you've just created is quite a temptation for any prowler looking for an easy snack.

John Shewey works around jetty habitats with an eerie sense of confidence. Watching that guy negotiate slippery rocks and cement blocks, you'd think he was half sea otter. And I'm right there with him! Our coastal forays usually include night sessions on some slime-covered, barnacle-encrusted, crab-festooned highway of riprap. Why? Because the rockfishing can be awesome! Oh sure, we'll work from floating docks tucked in quiet bays when we can, but the raucous world of open-coast jetties is always the most fun. With every cast, we never know what will try to murder our flies: rockfish, cabezons, and lingcod all have tried it at one time or another. It's a harsh world among the riprap, but there's also an extra dose of adrenaline as your offering disappears into the ink.

IT WAS THE THIRD DAY IN A ROW we were running with the whales. The Inside Passage was like glass, with nary a disturbance on the surface except from the humpback whales that fed on krill. What an amazing sight to behold—thirty-thousand-pound leviathans corralling prey through a cooperative feeding behavior known as bubble netting. The group of whales had circled the krill and had begun blowing bubbles from below. The "bubble net" buoyed and concentrated every living thing within it, trapping it beneath the surface, where the whales could then crash though the dense mass of food. Each time one of the humpbacks opened its cavernous mouth and extended the pleats in its throat, a salt-water river gushed in, carrying everything in the vicinity with it—plankton, krill, baitfish, all trapped in the flood.

The author shows a mint Alaskan silver.
PHOTOGRAPH BY GLENN KISHI

Captain Butcher's voice thundered: "Pick up the rods! Pick up the rods!" As a result of the whales' feeding frenzy, the surface was littered with stunned baitfish. All around us we could see silver flashes and swirls. Only this time it was Alaska's pink salmon that dined on the silvery bait. The entire surface was an explosion of whales, salmon, and their prey.

All I could think of was, "Who cares about fly fishing at a time like this?" When was the last time you could look down the throat of a live humpback whale just a few yards from the bow of your boat? The fishing could wait. I'd surely get another chance to cast to a wild salmon.

The whales finally gorged themselves and sounded into the abyss. Within moments, the surface returned to its placid state. As our skiff drifted closer to the kelp line, I noted a ripple not far off the stern. Then another appeared, and another, and finally a porpoising fish. The whales may have left, but the salmon were still there. It had taken less than twenty minutes to bring another school into range—and now I was ready to make my cast.

On another memorable afternoon, Josh Jones and I were working over a huge school of mint-silver cohos just north of Kasnyku Falls, and the session was a real screamfest. We were casting our flies over the salmon in about fifteen feet of crystalline water. Silvers were breaching all around us, and the cove boomed with every fish's effort. Perhaps the salmon felt a need to shake the sea lice anchored in their skin or loosen the female's eggs before spawning. I really couldn't tell you why they were airborne, but within the school, there were a large number of aggressive fish that had no problem eating our streamers. The action lasted for hours. One hookup after another had finally brought us both to our knees. The school had just plain worn us out! I remember Josh's smile. I remember my tired wrists. Salty salmon are a perfect match for flyrodding.

Pacific salmon are easily accessible in shallow saltwater habitats. Four of the five species—cohos (*Oncorhynchus kisutch*), pinks (*Oncorhynchus gorbuscha*), sockeyes (*Oncorhynchus nerka*), and chums (*Oncorhynchus keta*)—are common targets for wading anglers. Working along beaches, walking estuary flats, even casting from rocky points around kelp beds, fly fishers on foot routinely can target these favored gamefish. Of course, all five species, including the chinook salmon, are available to the boating angler. Though they might be found in shallow water, chinooks (*Oncorhynchus tshawytscha*) are more apt to be encountered in deeper inlets or water farther from shore.

As an anadromous fish, the salmon spends much of its life in the ocean. The actual time varies from species to species. Most of the fish are multiyear mariners. Their size and strength are a result of the time spent at sea. Pacific salmon are famous for their seafaring migrations, which in some cases total thousands of miles. Their ancient routes are pretty well defined, allowing scientists and anglers alike to anticipate their movements.

No matter which salmon species you pursue, an intermediate sinking line is the one to choose for estuaries and slow-moving water. For subsurface presentations, you couldn't ask for a better design. It's a great line for exploring calm surf, as well. I even use my intermediate line for top-water popper presentations. Additional sink-tip lines, Type III, IV, and V will allow you to drop your fly into deeper feeding lanes or negotiate faster currents. If you choose to work in bluewater conditions, which often require you to reach considerable depths and cope with even stronger, faster currents, you'll need the fastest-sinking designs you can find, 500-grains or heavier. Shooting heads or integrated shooting heads and running lines are the key to reaching deep-running fish.

PINKS

These salmon, also known as humpbacks or humpies, are available from the spring through the early fall. Boating is the ticket to early season success, while late July and August are especially productive for wading fly fishers. Pinks are typically fall spawners, with their offspring heading out to sea sometime during the spring and summer. The young salmon then average two years roaming the marine environment.

The life cycle of this species makes it a boom-or-bust spawner. One significant run exists in every river with a pink salmon run: odd-year and even-year spawners, and one or the other predominates. Returning populations can drop steeply during an off year in certain locations, since most of their on-year relatives are still out at sea. With a little homework, you can identify the spawning cycle of almost any local fishery you wish to explore. The majority of pinks appear to be odd-year spawners, if only because in the majority of rivers, odd-year spawners predominate.

These are fairly small salmon, and most caught on a fly rod will weigh from three to six pounds. Pinks of seven pounds or larger are caught, but infrequently.

These fish are predominantly silver. A blue accent along the back is common. Large oval spotting is characteristic on the back and on both lobes of the tail. As they near spawning grounds, the fish turn a dark olive-green on the back. Their sides also fade from bright silver to a muted gray-green.

Rods suited for this game are 6-weights and 7-weights. Line choices should include full intermediate sinking and Type III and IV sink-tip designs. Leaders should be fairly long, generally around nine feet overall, including tippet. The clearer the water, the longer your leader needs to be. Tippet strengths of 8 to 10 pounds are standard.

Fly patterns needn't be complicated. The fish appear to key on tiny euphausiids, other estuary shrimp, and krill. Pinks find pink patterns pretty. Hook sizes 4 and 6 are great all-around choices. I've experienced times when a size 8 was the hot fly. Think small, and think sparse. I carry a few pearlescent imitations as backup variations on the theme. Patterns such as the CDC Shrimp and the Diamond Shrimp are perfect for pinks.

Cohos

Cohos, also known as silvers, begin to appear in the late summer. August is consistently a landmark month. Peak spawning activity continues throughout the fall and into the early winter. Coho offspring average a year in their natal stream environment. Their sojourn at sea lasts two to four years. Most will reach maturity by the third year, triggering their return to their native streams.

Well-developed coho are hefty fish, typically running ten, twelve, even fifteen pounds, and fly fishers have legitimate shots at casting flies to silvers exceeding this range in many locations, especially in southeast Alaska's spectacular fisheries.

Coho are a beautiful metallic silver with a green-blue back. A series of small black spots occurs on the back, dorsal fin, and upper caudal fin. Another unique characteristic of this species is its white gum line.

The rods of choice for pursuing these powerful salmon are 9-weights and 10-weights. Line selections again include full intermediate sinking and sink-tip designs. Because silvers often run a bit deeper than pinks and in stronger currents, I recommend Type IV or faster-sinking lines. Shooting heads also will work and give you the flexibility to make deeper, bluewater presentations. Leader and tippet combinations are generally 9 feet or shorter. Tippet strengths of 12 to 15 pounds are highly recommended. I carry lighter tippets, though, in the event that ultrafine presentations are required.

Your collection of flies should concentrate on baitfish patterns. You can supplement those with small tidewater shrimp patterns such as the Horner Deer Hair Shrimp. The cornerstone baitfish are sand lances, herring, candlefish, and anchovies. Have your selection range in size. An ALF, Sea Habit, Fatal Attraction in green/chartreuse, Green Comet, Sorcerer's Touch, or Pearl Yeti between two and five inches long is a terrific choice. Using a slider or popper will also tempt aggressive fish to strike. The Salmon Waker, Pink Pollywog, and small foam sliders are my favorite top-water patterns.

SOCKEYES

Ounce for ounce and pound for pound, the sockeye, also known as the red or blueback salmon, is one of the toughest salmon species you can encounter. These are the only salmon that seek spawning habitat in and around lakes, however, and his requirement for very specific spawning drainages limits the salmon's distribution. Sockeye exhibit an inclination for lake shallows and adjacent streambed habitat, in particular inlets and outlets. Sockeye are summer spawners, and hence the season for them primarily is June and July.

Young sockeyes can spend up to three years inland before heading out to sea. Their ocean stay typically lasts from one to four years. They grow to an average weight of five to eight pounds, with larger fish caught every year. Fly fishers buttoned-up to a ten-pound sockeye will find the salmon a real test of skill and tackle. The sockeye's strength and stamina often will surprise you. Sockeyes sport a blue-green back and silver sides. The back is covered with fine black speckling. As they alter their appearance for spawning, the fish get green heads, red bodies, and yellowish fins.

I favor an 8-weight outfit for these great gamefish. Your line selection should be the same as for pink salmon: full intermediate sinking and Type III and IV sink-tip designs. Tippet strengths of 8 to 10 pounds are again standard choices. Most leaders are 7 feet or shorter, tippet included.

Sockeyes feed heavily on smaller baitfish and shrimp. The flies I choose are attractor patterns that are variations of steelhead flies: a Green or Gold Comet, the Sockeye Boss, and the Sockeye Special, sizes 2 through 8. For shrimp imitations, I use Deer Hair Shrimp, Diamond Shrimp, and CDC Shrimp.

CHUMS

You might find chums, also known as dog salmon, as early as June or as late as October. Much depends on the individual population. Peak spawning activity begins in July and continues through fall in most locations. Chums are true seafaring creatures. Their migrations are some of the most extensive along the Pacific coastline. These hearty salmon travel the briny wilderness for up to five years. Fish of twelve to fifteen pounds are the norm, but fly fishers could find themselves tangling with a bulldogging trophy approaching twenty pounds.

Chum salmon are silver, with a steel-blue back. They lack the spotting found on other salmon. This species, however, does have black tips on all fins except the dorsal. As the fish matures, most acquire a series of blotches on their sides, irregular vertical bars that are dark red or purple.

The rods most often used for chums range from 8-weights to 10-weights. You'll appreciate the heavier tackle if you find these fish under bluewater conditions. I use the same line and leader selection I use for cohos: Type IV or faster-sinking lines or shooting heads, leaders of 9 feet or shorter, and tippet strengths from 12 to 15 pounds, with lighter tippet material in reserve.

Fly patterns once again either imitate baitfish or are general attractors. Tidewater shrimp imitations should supplement the collection, though. Most of the successful fly fishers I know use smaller patterns when targeting chums. They prefer streamers no longer than three inches, including ALFs, Comets, Fatal Attractions, and Pearl Yetis, tied on hooks from size 2 to size 1/0. They're all proven winners.

CHINOOKS

The chinook salmon, also known as the king, tyee, and blackmouth, is indeed the king of the salmon. It's the largest salmon in the Pacific. The chinook may be found near its natal waters at any time from the spring through

The legacy continues.
PHOTOGRAPH BY GLENN KISHI

the fall. It varies from location to location, so you need to do a bit of research before heading out on any adventure. You wouldn't want to assume a spring spawn, only to find out that you've chosen a destination with fall-run fish. If I had to roll the dice, however, I'd bet most populations spawn earlier in the season.

The chinook's ocean odyssey begins fairly soon after hatching. It takes at least four to five years for a chinook to attain its impressive size. Fish of fifteen to thirty pounds are common catches for sport anglers. The record freshwater specimen, caught in the Kenai River, in Alaska, was over ninety pounds. I've seen numerous fly-caught chinook well over twenty pounds. Both bluewater and estuary specimens will be sure to test your mettle.

Saltwater kings are generally silver, with a green-blue back. Their most distinguishing marks are the large, irregular spots along the back, dorsal fin, and entire caudal fin. They also have a dark, often black, gum line.

Heavy rods, ten-weight outfits or heavier, are highly recommended for this game. Remember, these are big fish and usually are found in big water. Shooting heads are the real ticket here. If you're a bluewater angler, the heavier the head, the better the performance, and 500-grain or lead-core heads frequently are employed. Estuary fly fishers should consider working with standard sink-tips, Type III, IV, or V, or longer shooting heads of 200 to 300 grains. Leaders are usually no more than 6 feet overall. Tippet breaking strengths may vary from 12 to 18 pounds. It's best to be prepared for all conditions.

Large baitfish imitations are without a doubt the flies of choice. Herring, anchovies, and sand lances are dominant forage fish. Bluewater anglers should also carry along squid imitations. Streamers from three to six inches long are about right, tied on hooks from size 2 to size 4/0. Once the salmon enter shallower estuary habitats, smaller attractor patterns and shrimp imitations become key elements for success.

Chinooks are considered the most difficult species to entice with a fly; so gear up for the challenge and get ready for hard work. The king of the Pacific sets the rules!

THE PREDAWN FOG HAD LAID CLAIM to the coast, enveloping the estuary and muffling all sound. I felt like I was standing in a place without boundaries. A gentle surf tugged at my legs, luring me further into the marine world, a place I hold dear. I took another step and made another cast.

Glenn Kishi was wading the flat with me. There couldn't have been more than fifty feet between us. I turned just in time to see the water shudder and a large mud cloud rise to the sur-

California halibut are rapidly becoming a target for fly fishers.
PHOTOGRAPH BY GLENN KISHI

face. Glenn had startled a halibut. A mere twenty feet away, directly between us, the fish had been holding in less than three feet of water. We both saw the halibut's path as the surface revealed its undulating flight. I hadn't retrieved my fly from the previous cast, and suddenly I felt a sharp jolt. Another rap immediately followed as baitfish broke through the surface and scattered like confetti. The halibut had fled through the school and had taken my streamer. Then it was gone. I waded into deeper water and made another cast.

There was a wind seam to Glenn's right, and I thought more bait could be moving through that area. He made a cast to the outer edge of the seam and let his fly drop into the tapering basin beneath. When he sensed a resistance during his retrieve, his initial thought was he had just hooked more seaweed. Nevertheless, because you never really know what will happen when you're fishing the Pacific, he used a strip strike to try to set the hook. The line simply felt heavy, but he struck a second and third time. Three's a charm, and Glenn was rewarded with a bucking rod tip. He put pressure on the fish and began to walk back toward shallower water. With every step Glenn took, I had a clear view of the mottled brown back of the fish. The lapping surf wasn't any more than a foot deep at this point. His treasure was a California halibut that weighed a solid eight to ten pounds.

They may have been incidental catches in times past by fly fishers angling in salt water, but flatfish now have become a legitimate fly-fishing target. Anglers from Alaska to Baja are enjoying the unique challenge of fishing for flatties in shallow water. Two species in particular are prime examples for flyrodding fun: the starry flounder (*Platichthys stellatus*), and Glenn's catch, the California halibut (*Paralichthys californicus*). Estuary fly fishers will find these sport fish ambushing prey on the flats or from deepwater pockets. Surf-zone anglers can target them in calm troughs or in scoured-out pools along sandy points. Both of these game-fish frequent habitats with sand or mud substrata. The halibut favors sandy niches whenever available. Depending on the characteristics of your local waters, flatfish can be accessible to just about any fly fisher, afoot or afloat.

The starry flounder is perhaps the widest-ranging species of the two, but not by much. It simply has the ability to withstand lower salinity levels. It's the smaller gamefish, with three-foot specimens about as big as they get. Maximum weights tend to be around twenty pounds. Fly fishers usually encounter smaller fish weighing in the two-to-six-pound range.

Starry flounders belong to the Pleuronectidae family. These flatfish are right-eyed: they have their eyes on the right side of the dorsal fin. However, the starry flounder is a unique species in that family because it can be either right-eyed or left-eyed. A more significant identifying feature is the flounder's dark bars on the dorsal, anal, and caudal fins. The bar coloring alternates from black to a dusty yellow-orange. The fish's back is predominately brown, with irregular black highlights.

The starry flounder typically spawns around February, March, and April. That's when you'll find them predominantly in shallow-water environments. The farther you travel south along our coastline, the earlier the spawning begins.

Starry flounders have fairly small mouths. Their diet consists of crustaceans, worms, baitfish, and even soft-shelled clams. Fly patterns in the one-to-three-inch range work well. The Pearl Yeti, Surf Grub, Jay's Grass Shrimp, and small Clouser Minnows are fine choices. Recommended hooks are size 2, 4, and 6.

The California halibut is quite a bit larger than its cousin. It can grow to five feet and attain weights well into the sixty-pound range. You'll most likely encounter fish weighing from five to twenty pounds, however. A member of the Bothidae family, they're categorized with left-eyed flatfish, but like starry flounders, California halibut can be both left-eyed and right-eyed. The halibut's back is mottled in darker browns, black, and ashen gray. Blotching occurs on the back and fins. Be aware that these critters have a substantial set of needle-sharp teeth. That's a clue that they feed heavily on baitfish.

Anchovies, smelt, grunions, and sardines are top items on their

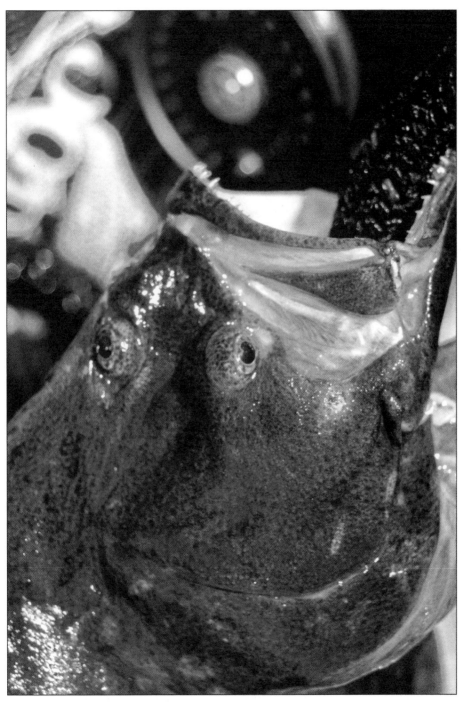

Halibut come equipped with needle-sharp teeth for capturing prey.
PHOTOGRAPH BY GLENN KISHI

menus. Halibut also target young bass, perch, and a variety of crustaceans. Imitations from two to six inches long are appropriate. Deceivers, ALFs, and Gold Buccaneers will do the job. Hook sizes can vary from 2 to 3/0.

California halibut spawn from April through July. It's during this time that you'll find them frequenting depths of twenty feet or less. Flats with an average depth of two to five feet are often ideal for spawning flat-fish. This is especially true if the flat is situated near a deepwater channel.

All of the flatfish species are supreme ambush predators and camou-flage specialists. Not only do they hide in the substratum, they can alter their color patterns to blend into their surroundings. They accomplish this by manipulating pigment cells and reflector cells in their skins. Flatfish transmit visual information about their surroundings through brain signals to activate the skin cells. The pigment cells match the color, patterning, and to some degree even the texture of the places they choose to wait in ambush. The reflector cells, located deeper in the skin, are actu-ally loaded with tiny crystals that reflect light. The combination of cells activated creates the perfect match to blend into the surrounding habitat.

Flounders and halibut are creatures of the benthic zone, living near or on the bottom. So fly fishers should present their offerings low and slow, mimicking any prey species cruising near bottom structure or cover. California halibut routinely take prey from the middle of the water column, however, and surf-zone halibut have been known to break the surface in pursuit of baitfish. Anglers targeting this species therefore can anticipate a strike anywhere along the fly pattern's retrieve path.

The rod weights and lines to use will vary from protected estuary environments to the turbulent surf zone. In calmer conditions, I recom-mend an 8-weight outfit. In the heavy currents, crashing breakers, and cutting winds of the outer coastline, a 9-weight or 10-weight is more apt to let you control your presentations.

Surf-zone anglers should build their outfits around fast-sinking lines or shooting heads. You'll see both integrated shooting heads and running lines and traditional shooting-head systems in use. I prefer to work with a thirty-foot shooting head in this case. The running line is either a 35-pound flat-beam PVC or uncoated hard monofilament. The small diameter of these materials helps the running line cut through the water column.

The terminal rigging for a surf presentation is pretty straightforward. You don't need to taper the leader. A straight piece of 12-pound to 16-pound tippet material is fine. I've sometimes used a short bite trace, a foot of 20-pound mono, to help combat the abrasiveness of the beach environment. The overall length of my rig is usually around 7 feet. If con-ditions are rougher than I first expected, I might reduce my leader's length to as little as 4 feet. I'll do what ever it takes to keep my fly in con-tact with the sandy bottom.

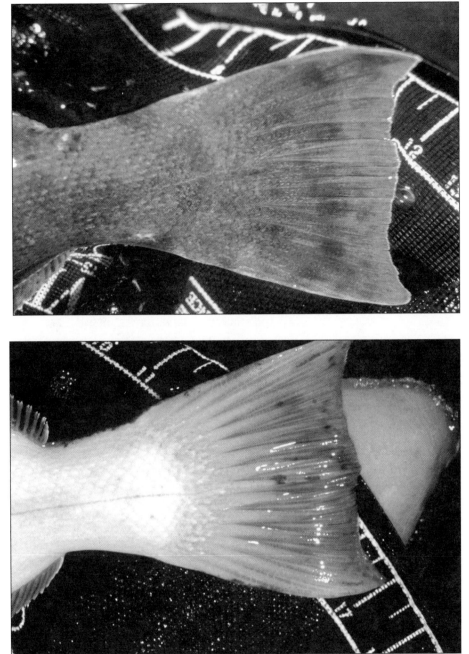

Flatfish tail comparison: top is mottled by pigment cells and reflector cells.
PHOTOGRAPH BY GLENN KISHI

Flatfish tail comparison: underside has no need for color or patterning.
PHOTOGRAPH BY GLENN KISHI

Estuary fly fishers are faced with a completely different set of circumstances. The flatfish could be lurking in extremely clear and shallow water. When I work flats, my line of choice is a clear intermediate striper line. It gives me wonderful depth control during a long retrieve. The clear line may even provide with a higher degree of stealth, as well. My leader and tippet combination is longer and lighter for this scenario. Most often, I rig up with a 10-pound or 12-pound tippet without a shock trace if at all possible. Stealthy presentations are the goal in this environment. If I feel like I'm lining fish, my backup spool is rigged with a sink-tip line with a floating running line.

A growing number of Southern California anglers are finding success with regular floating lines and long, light leaders. I believe their tackle innovations could also produce for Pacific Northwest fly fishers working the shallow tidal flats of many salmon rivers.

If you'll be exploring deep-water channels, heavier shooting heads are once again the tackle of choice. The idea is to cut through the heavy current and drop your fly into the strike zone at the bottom. As I already mentioned, if you can find a shallow area adjacent to one of these channels, you could be in for some terrific action. The channel is a highway for baitfish and predators alike. Even without baitfish in abundance, the flatfish can slide onto the flats and forage among the shell beds or patches of eelgrass with ease.

Whether you fish shallow habitats or deepwater haunts, the style for retrieving your fly won't change much. The tempo is basically slow, with long, steady pulls. Incorporating a few short pauses between pulls repositions the fly to disrupt a bit of sand or mud on the ensuing retrieve. This small disturbance might lend an extra attention-grabbing element to your presentation.

There's yet another flatfish experience for those of you seeking to push the envelope. Anglers working Alaskan fisheries are experimenting with true deepwater presentations for Pacific halibut. These fish are the denizens of the deep. Most sport anglers drop jigs down hundreds of feet into the cold-water abysses of the north. Fly fishers are instead targeting the younger halibut that frequent shallower habitats. "Shallow" in this case still means depths of forty to sixty feet, on average.

The adult Alaskan halibut spawn during the winter. This mainly takes place in deep water. Young halibut enter shallower water in the spring. Nursery habitats generally include protected coves and small bays with sandy bottoms.

Northern Pacific halibut dine on squid, fish, crabs, and clams. Large flies are the ticket to enticing these gamefish. The bigger the fly you can cast, the better your chances of success.

The best lines to work with are shooting heads constructed from the lead-core line known as LC-13. Its small diameter and extreme weight will sink the fly deep and fast. Mono or PVC running line also will cut through the water with a minimum of resistance and help sink the fly. If you opt for an integrated shooting head and running line, consider one rated at between 650 and 800 grains. These lines have large-diameter heads and coated running lines, however. They'll get your fly down, it just takes a bit longer—particularly in heavy currents. As for your leader, keep it short and stout. Four feet of 18-pound or twenty-pound tippet material is perfect.

Rods for these deepwater presentations should be 10-weights or heavier. You'll be required to work against bigger fish at extreme depths. Expect to engage in a lot of lifting and leveraging. True deepwater halibut are heroic in size, and equally epic in strength.

Dan Williams with a
California striped bass.
PHOTOGRAPH BY KEN HANLEY

HISTORY COUNTS. History especially counts in fly fishing, a sport with a long and proud heritage. You might think fly fishing in salt water is a recent development, but you'd be wrong. From what I can find out, one of the first fly-caught saltwater stripers in California was taken around 1925 by Jules Cuerin in San Francisco Bay. Cuerin is also credited as one of the inspirations for Russell Chatham's striper explorations of the 1950s. Chatham went on to become recognized as the first fly fisher to take a striped bass within the Pacific's surf zone. He continued to expand his efforts at saltwater fly fishing throughout the region north of the Golden Gate. Others were soon to follow, including Bob Nauheim and Bill Schaadt. Other pioneers centered their attention on the central and southern parts of San Francisco Bay. In the 1960s, Dan Blanton, Larry Green, Gary Dyer, Ed Given, Bob Edgely, and Lawrence Summers were some of the folks who explored this vast stretch of water. The tackle and techniques they developed have become essentials for legions of Western fly fishers today. But the quest continues to refine both to take best advantage of the West Coast striper fisheries. I'm proud to carry on the legacy of those spirited individuals who preceded me. They've provided me with a real sense of place.

Stripers weren't always here. Like many of the fly fishers pursuing them, they're descendants of immigrants. The original stock was shipped west on the railroad to be put on display as a curiosity at the state fair and introduced into San Francisco Bay in 1879. Since they were here, someone decided to see if they would thrive in the bay environment. The initial stocking took place with a mere 132 fish. A supplemental stocking three years later included only 300 specimens. Those are pretty modest numbers to have created such a wonderful fishery. Striped bass may be indigenous to the eastern seaboard, but they found California waters an easy place to which to adapt. The bay's expansive habitat was a natural corridor between the Pacific's food-rich inshore environments and the favorable spawning grounds available in the Sacramento/San Joaquin River Delta complex. The entire system was a perfect setting for stripers to proliferate. In addition, the kelp beds and protected coves on California's northern coastline provided additional habitat, and striped bass were on the move north within the first ten years of being introduced into San Francisco Bay. The offspring of these fish entered Oregon's Coos Bay region circa 1914. Populations continued to spread, both naturally and by planting, until today, you can encounter striped bass from Washington's Columbia River drainage to California's southernmost estuarine habitats.

Development has taken its toll on the Golden State's striper fisheries, but California's bass are still recognized as the premiere fishery for West Coast fly fishers. The most viable saltwater populations continue to be found in California and south-central Oregon. In addition to the fishery in the San Francisco Bay Area, there's an increasing presence of stripers in Southern California from Santa Barbara down into Newport Bay. With limited distribution north of California, Northwest anglers have the best opportunity to discover this terrific gamefish in Oregon's Winchester Bay complex, which drains the Umpqua River.

Striped bass (*Morone saxatilis*) have such a distinct shape and color it's pretty hard to confuse them with other bass in Western waters. If you're used to conjuring up images of largemouth bass, you'll be surprised by the length-to-thickness ratio of a striper. These beauties are typically at least three times as long as they are thick. Dark above (ranging from olive to dark blue), metallic on the flanks (sporting numerous rows of jet black as an accent), and almost snow white on the belly, these are striking gamefish. Their huge golden eyes are the crowning touch.

The stripes of individual fish project tantalizing patterns, each unique. Irregularities cause illusions of quilting, checkerboard squares, or even a heavy dripping effect. It all just adds to the wonderment.

All stripers have a conspicuous fin structure. Their dorsal and caudal fins are thick-rayed sails designed to maneuver around cover and in heavy currents. With a deep-notched V, their dorsal appears to be two fins, the forward part stiffened by prominent spines.

Virtually all stripers develop into mature spawning stock within two to six years. Males spawn around their second year, while females typically won't reach maturity until their fourth. This means that females spawning for the first time average four pounds or heavier, while the

Dan Blanton hits a home run during "the World Series bite" in San Francisco Bay.
PHOTOGRAPH BY KEN HANLEY

equivalent males are much smaller, approximately one pound. Spawning occurs in fresh water during the spring. Then they move back out through the bays and estuaries to salt water.

Saltwater anglers therefore have the maximum chance for action beginning in the late spring and on through the autumn. Estuary fly fishers also get their first shots at migrating fish leaving their freshwater spawning grounds in the late spring. Entering the large bay systems from fresh water, the fish concentrate along shoreline cover, built or natural, on flats, and at the edges of deeper channels. These fish are strictly transient. They follow bait populations and feed while in the bay, however their ultimate goal is the Pacific, where they feed heavily in the surf zone and in the protected shoreline habitat. July, August, and September are the prime months for chasing stripers along the outer coast. Then, beginning in early fall, the bulked-up stripers return to the bays on their way back to their spawning grounds. In my home waters, a terrific bite occurs around baseball's major-league play-offs. We call it "the World Series bite." Fishing any lower bay region around tidal creeks and flats can be extremely productive during this time. As the autumn progresses, the stripers continue to move inland, into the intricate Delta waterways and large river basins that house the bass while they prepare to spawn. That makes the winter months the time for freshwater striper angling.

Pacific saltwater stripers feed primarily on sardines, anchovies, smelt, herring, surf perch, various crabs, and shrimp. Other common forage includes a variety of marine worms and bivalves. Your fly collection should begin with baitfish imitations. You're sure to encounter schooling bait, no matter where you travel for stripers. Streamers as small as two inches or as large as six inches tied on hook sizes from size 2 through 4/0 will cover the spectrum perfectly. Clouser Minnows, Sea Habits, Flashtail Whistlers, and ALFs are top-producing patterns. Don't forget to add a few poppers and sliders for top-water fireworks.

If you find yourself on the water without encountering any activity from schooling baitfish, it's time to turn to imitations of the other foods that stripers favor. At least half a dozen species of crabs and shrimp inhabit the bays, estuaries, and shoreline habitat. Species of note include the Pacific mole crab, the purple shore crab, the Oregon cancer crab, young Dungeness crabs, grass shrimp, and beach or bay ghost shrimp. Effective crustacean imitations are typically two to four inches in length, tied on hooks from size 2 to 6. Try my Labyrinth Crab and Jay's Grass Shrimp, for starters.

Often overlooked, but no less important, worms are a favorite fare of striped bass from the Atlantic to the Pacific. Atlantic fly fishers well know the importance of the "cinder worm hatch." Our Western waters play host to four significant species: red *Lineus* worms, on rocky shores and beaches; tufted-gilled blood worms, on beaches and in bays and estuaries; clam worms, on rocky shores and in bays and estuaries; and six-lined nemerteans, on rocky shores

The red Lineus *and other worms are prime edibles in the striped bass diet.*
PHOTOGRAPH BY GLENN KISH

and around wharves, docks, and pilings. These slimy bass treats offer prime forage from the churning surf zone to quiet inner bays. Some of these creatures can stretch well beyond a foot in length. As a practical matter, fly fishers generally work with smaller imitations, from four to six inches long.

Surf-zone anglers should concentrate on red *Lineus* and tufted-gilled worm imitations from dark red or brown to olive and pink. Bay and estuary fly fishers would do well with a pattern in the clam worm's colors, iridescent green and blue, with a bit of red or gold for an accent. This is an especially productive choice around thick eelgrass beds. An imitation of the six-lined nemertean, with its alternating black and white bands, is terrific for fishing any built environment. Patterns such as Andy Burk's V-Worm or an assortment of Woolly Buggers will meet the needs for wormin' stripers.

Striper rods should be capable of doing heavy duty. You're targeting an amazingly strong gamefish. You're often presenting bulky, wind-resistant flies. Weighted patterns are standard. Blustery winds and strong currents come with the territory. That means 9-weight or 10-weight rods are pretty much the choice for bay and estuarine waters. In the surf, 10-weight and perhaps even heavier rods are the key for effectively working in the conditions you'll encounter there. Your rod should offer you great control in leveraging or lifting these hearty gamefish from cover and from fast or deep waters.

Line choice depends on the specific habitat you'll be fishing as you follow the striper migrations from freshwater to saltwater environments and back again. For exploring shallows such as grass beds, flats, tidal creeks, and sloughs, try a full intermediate sinking or floating striper line. Slow-sinking shooting heads are another fine option in fairly shallow waters. If your adventures take you into deeper waters, such as channels and protected coves, then fast-sinking shooting heads are required. Traditional shooting heads are the norm for Western fly fishers in these circumstances, with Types 4 and 6 the most commonly used, but straight lead-core LC-13 is the shooting head of choice under extreme conditions. Those preferring integrated shooting heads and running lines, such as the Rio, Teeny, or Orvis designs, would do best with lines rated at 400 or 500 grains. Surf-zone anglers find an intermediate sinking line a great choice for popper work and subsurface streamers. Deeper presentations are again accomplished with fast-sinking shooting heads.

Leader and tippet combinations are short and stout. Most anglers don't even taper their terminal tackle, and 6 feet overall seems to be the magic length for most conditions. Breaking strengths of 12 or 16 pounds are recommended. Carry a few lighter tippets and give yourself the opportunity to adapt if necessary. Another option is to incorporate a twelve-inch shock trace of 20-pound or 25-pound-test material, which is prudent around abrasive riprap or other built cover. A growing number of Westerners prefer to use a straight 20-pound leader around heavy cover. It's really your choice.

Fly fishers stalk striped bass either by looking for signs that fish are feeding or by blind casting into premiere habitat. Diving birds, skipping baitfish, surface swirls, V wakes, and what look like dark balls moving subsurface, indicating baitfish are being pushed or herded by predators, are all signs something is feeding down there—and that something may well be a striper. So are "breezing" baitfish. When being pursued, they sometimes break the surface in a wave that looks like a breeze ruffling the water, with the fish in the rear jumping over the whole group in their efforts to escape. More subtle signs include shuddering grass tips or mud clouds rising to the surface. Before you fish any striper habitat, know which of these signs are to be expected most often.

Without any visual tips on feeding activity, you have to cast blind to productive water. That means you need ways to narrow your choices, because there's always more unproductive water than you expect. Concentrate on major current seams, ambush points around built and natural cover, and deepwater edges. Areas with moving water should take precedent.

The striped bass is a supreme night predator. Its eyes have extremely large pupils that favor prowling in low-light conditions. Fishing along jetties or even wading estuary flats can be incredibly productive during these hours. If this isn't practical (or legal), I'd recommend fishing either the predawn or sunset hours. I'm not saying daylight conditions won't produce positive results, but you generally will find yourself working harder for those rewards.

Day or night, tides are a critical factor triggering striper movement. The tide's natural rhythm dictates baitfish dispersal and affords the striper access to flooded structure. You'll have to do a little research to discover the best tide cycle to follow. Each location you explore has specific requirements for maximum potential. In some cases, it will be the quarter-moon phase that keeps hungry stripers active on shallow flats, or feeding close in the breaking surf, or cruising along a fertile kelp line. In others, the new-moon or full-moon phases might provide swifter currents along jetty walls and flood tidal creeks or sloughs. As part of your investigations, you'll also discover when the hot action occurs in relation to the incoming and outgoing phases of the tides. Local knowledge of tidal influence is the ultimate power in decision making for the successful salty fly fisher.

Blue shark adventures are the perfect big-game training ground.
PHOTOGRAPH BY KEN HANLEY

GROWING UP NEAR PETE'S HARBOR was nothing short of a great adventure, especially for those of us who had the privilege of meeting Fritz. His home was a dilapidated shanty on the slough. This guy was a simple sailor. If he could smell salt in the air, he was in heaven. Fritz was a real character—a modern-day Sinbad. His tales about seafaring voyages to distant lands were pure magic for a kid. His knowledge of fishing the bay was uncanny. He had the touch. . . . Fritz could fish.

The first time I saw a shark was on the end of Fritz's line. That was back around 1965. Today, I'm still just as fascinated by these mysterious and beautiful creatures. During the summer of 1989, I began to tangle with these fish on a fly rod.

Blue sharks roaming Monterey Bay were my first targets. I'd heard of the wild shark-fishing adventures of the San Jose Fly Casters. Bob Edgeley and Lawrence Summers are credited with the first explorations of this fishery. Their success rate was well-known among many of the Bay Area fly fishers. After reading a few articles and running into some of the club members participating in those shark-fishing excursions, I was ready to assemble my tackle and head out the door.

When I did, Hall Kelley and I shared some great moments on the water. After Hall caught his first blue shark, fly fishing would never be the same for him.

That day, we had established a chum line to lure the sharks to within casting distance. The oily remnants of salmon, rockfish, and sardines were combined with bread crumbs and sand. The sand helped to drop the chum a few feet under the surface, just out of the range of scavenger gulls. We also had a salmon head secured to a throw line, and as a blue shark worked its way up the slick, we threw the salmon head about twenty feet off our stern. Then we employed the classic bait-'n'-switch tactic. Hall cast his streamer as our captain simultaneously pulled in the salmon head. The shark immediately swung to the fly. Hall let it drift a moment. I'm sure that instant seemed an eternity. With the subtlety of a midge-sipping trout, the big predator took the fly. There was no explosive movement, no thrashing about. As the shark wheeled away from the boat,

Hall reared back on the rod while at the same time setting the hook with his stripping hand, and it clearly took hold in the corner of the mouth. That blue accelerated like a fighter jet beginning a strafing run. Every fiber in the rod Hall held was put to the test. Alternating between blistering surface runs and spiraling descents to extreme depths, that blue shark redefined what fly fishing could be all about for Hall that day.

The blue shark (*Prionace glauca*) is one of the few members of the Requiem family found in colder waters. They average six feet in length and approximately sixty to eighty pounds. These magnificent creatures are cobalt blue above and snow white below. Their shape is indeed like a fighter jet's, long and sleek. They look like the craft flown by the Navy's precision team, the Blue Angels. The creature's head is narrow and pointed, offering a surface area that produces little resistance. Its pectoral fins and caudal fin (particularly the top lobe) are long and stiff, perfectly adapted for high-speed maneuvering. The tail is an asymmetrical design that creates significant lift, as well as forward propulsion. The shark's pectoral fins and front underbody form a flattened hydrofoil surface that also creates lift. The blue shark lacks a swim bladder and consequently doesn't have the ability to hover, so it needs this lift to maintain balance and position.

Blues feed primarily on salmon, anchovies, sardines, and mackerel. Squid are another principal food resource. A simple fly collection consisting of white Deceivers, white-and-red Flashtail Whistlers, and a squid pattern is all you need to be successful. Some anglers prefer to augment this group with Deceivers tied in a combination of brown and red. I believe it depends, in large part, on what kind of chum you deploy. Hook sizes range from 4/0 to 6/0. The shark's teeth are serrated, so using a bite trace is highly recommended. Both wire and heavy mono bite traces are commonly used.

Rods with backbone, 10-weights through 13-weights, provide the leverage necessary to bring in these great gamefish. Sinking shooting heads coupled to intermediate-sinking running lines are what most anglers prefer. Leaders are usually 9 feet or shorter, overall. Use tough, abrasion-resistant material when you build or buy your leader.

Blues start showing up in numbers when the surface temperatures approach sixty degrees. The summer and early autumn are the peak months for this fishery. The range of the blue shark extends up and down the entire Pacific coastline.

If the large blue sharks of open bay waters aren't quite what you're looking for, there certainly are other fish in the shark family that are more easily

*Leopard sharks can offer
estuary anglers big thrills.*
PHOTOGRAPH BY HALL KELLEY

found. They often roam the shallows of estuaries, over sandy and rock-laden flats, or near the tide pool shelves of small coves. Leopard sharks (*Triakis semifasciata*), and smoothhound sharks (*Mustelus henlei*, the brown smoothhound, and *Mustelus californicus*, the gray smoothhound) are tremendous gamefish on light tackle from Oregon to Baja.

We're still in the process of experimenting with this fishery. One of my partners in this experiment was the late Captain Jim Flannery, a specialist in shark excursions. Our adventures throughout the San Francisco Bay complex have provided the refinements of technique and tackle I now use, but the experimentation continues. Join the fun!

Leopard sharks are found throughout the shallow-water environment all year long, but the late spring through the middle of the autumn is the peak period for flyrodders to seek them out. Waiting for the Thanksgiving weekend might be a stretch. The onset of showers does more than dampen the day: leopard sharks have a low tolerance for freshwater environments, and after a healthy rain, they head for more hospitable hangouts.

Leopard sharks dine mainly on small fish and invertebrates. The brown smoothhound shows a preference for crabs and shrimp. Both sharks find it hard to refuse a succulent squid. All these food items are easily represented with a fly. Both of these hunters are bottom feeders, with rows of small, sharp-edged teeth with blunt cusps that are well positioned for trapping and crushing prey, unlike many of the large pelagic sharks, with their long, triangular, pointed teeth with serrated edges and curved cusps.

These sharks are constantly on the move, roaming the mud flats and rocky shorelines in schools. More often than not, sharks of the same size school together. The males generally run about three to five feet in length. Females are larger. Sharks have cartilage, rather than bony skeletons, and the lack of a stiff bone structure gives these creatures the ability to turn on a dime. This extreme flexibility allows the leopard and smoothhound sharks to prowl effectively in tight cover.

A common misconception is that the leopard shark is as blind as a bat. On the contrary, its eyes adjust to light and sense movement quite well. There's no doubt that the leopard shark has highly developed sensory organs. Its lateral line provides excellent detection of low-frequency noise. The olfactory system is legendary in all sharks. Beyond that, they possess a fascinating series of organs in the skin. Located around the head are tiny pores filled with a gelatinous substance, the cells of which are lined with fine, hairlike sensors. These cells assist in identifying electrical currents. At close range, they can pick up the bioelectric field of another animal, which certainly is a handy little trick for hunting tasty morsels hidden in the sand and mud.

Currents ranging from one and a half knots to three knots induce the sharks to roam and feed. So fly-fishing success comes from fishing moving water. Choose a tide and location where the currents are slow enough to allow you to control the depth at which you present your offering, though. Currents of four knots or faster also stir and suspend an abundance of mud, possibly interfering with easy fly detection by the sharks. Incoming and outgoing tides both are productive. The slack times between tides are not.

The majority of sharks you're likely to catch will weigh between five and ten pounds. Standard 7-weight, 8-weight, or 9-weight saltwater outfits can handle these fish. Select a rod with which you're not afraid to get aggressive. If you happen to tag a larger leopard, it will wage a wicked dogfight with you. Shooting-head systems have brought me good fortune. Casting is the least of your worries. The key here is getting your offering down to the fish and keeping it there long enough to be eaten.

The leopard's sandpaper skin and raspy teeth could play havoc with your leader. I build mine to 6 feet in overall length with a 20-pound butt section, 12-pound tippet, and a short 30-pound mono bite trace. Does the shock trace make it sound a bit overbuilt? Probably, but it's cheap insurance. These fish are noted for excessive rolling and thrashing, and their abrasive skin can cut through leader material.

Fly patterns should imitate squid and the usual small baitfish, plus the plainfin midshipman, since this species is a principal target for estuary sharks. Unlike the silvery baitfish of the sea, it displays a combination of black, brown, and "butter" colors. Since the sharks respond to vibration so well, it's critical to offer a full-bodied fly that really pushes water when retrieved. In addition, the fly has to mimic the size or silhouette of the sharks' favorite prey. The Sea Arrow Squid, yellow Whistler, white Whistler, and blue-and-white Deceiver have caught a fair number of sharks for me. Most of the flies were on 2/0 hooks, although the squid was dressed on a 4/0. But I also know of many anglers who prefer to fish small shrimp patterns.

It took some experimenting to figure out where to find leopard sharks. They don't graph well (I'm told it has something to do with their swim bladders), so we've been far more successful using electronics to find the kinds of location where we've learned we can catch fish, rather than to find individual fish. We found it productive to work near breakwaters and where channels meet flats. Twenty feet is about as deep as we fish, with depths of twelve to fifteen feet the most effective. In San Francisco Bay, we've had extraordinary luck along the Alameda rock wall during the autumn. During the early summer, when spawning activity of the plainfin midshipmen begins to peak, Richardson Bay has been especially productive adjacent to the deeper channel of Raccoon Straits.

We've tried to take advantage of the gregarious nature of the male leopard sharks. They're well known for congregating in the shallows in schools of impressive numbers. Throw in a few smoothhounds, and the potential for action increases dramatically.

Like most fish, these sharks prefer to face into the prevailing current. Roll casting the line "upstream" not only helps the fly cut through the water column, it helps deliver the fly at the proper depth with the current. We like to hold the fly hovering against the current. It gives the fish ample time to home in on the target in turbid waters.

Leopard sharks are notorious for playing with their food. Conventional-tackle technique is to let them pick up the bait and run with it with the baitcasting reel in free spool before setting the hook. That's what I was brought up with, and that's what I began doing. It cost me quite a few fish. Quick sets, instead, put the fish on the fly line. The difference in hook styles is the key factor. Fly patterns are dressed on hooks with much shorter shanks than bait hooks have. Instead of the shark having to reposition the larger hook and bait in its mouth, it could decide to reject the fly immediately.

Recently, we've begun to explore the idea of using a chum line to attract leopard sharks. I'm not sure it's made any difference, but it probably hasn't hurt. We've noticed that when the chum basket rides high in the water column, it tends to draw the interest of bat rays, instead of leopard sharks. In fact, we've had trouble keeping the rays off our fly. These graceful creatures have amazing power in their wings, and the pressure they can exert really puts your equipment to the test.

Another area for encounters with small sharks is the surf zone. As more fly fishers work the surf, leopards are becoming the surprise catches of the day. The sharks often patrol the calmer troughs, looking for tumbling, disoriented prey. Anglers have reported increasing numbers of hookups in the evening and predawn hours. Surf-zone fly fishers exploring the southern reaches of the Pacific Coast, from central California south into to Baja, account for most of these reports.

Brian Hastings, for example, hooked into the largest leopard he'd ever seen while he was wading the surf along the Santa Barbara coast. He found the fish while hosting a fly-rod adventure for a friend who'd flown in from Australia. Standing thigh-deep in a gentle surf, Brian and his partner saw five sharks circling in the trough just a few feet ahead of their casting position. Hastings made his presentation, and the largest shark of the school turned to the fly. Though he's an accomplished angler, once Brian set the hook, he quickly lost control of the situation. His light surfperch outfit wasn't enough to handle this prize catch. He tried to run after the shark, but to no avail. The leopard was headed around a rocky point for deeper water. Brian finally pointed his rod directly toward the fish, clamped down on his spool, and simply waited for the tippet to separate.

Someday, somebody is going figure out how to find, catch, and then actually land these bad boys regularly. When that happens—Hooeee! We've caught and tussled with enough sharks in recent years to indicate we're on the right track. Afoot or afloat, you've got your hands full with these powerful, graceful adversaries.

The author shows the fin structure of a spotted sand bass.

PHOTOGRAPH BY GLENN KISHI

SPOTTED SAND BASS ARE ONE of my favorite fly-rod saltwater targets. They're also a favorite of "Pietro" Piconi. I never miss the chance to spend a day with Captain Pete on Mission Bay near San Diego, chasing his home-town spotties. A typical adventure is loaded with laughter, killer burritos, great weather, and of course plenty of tugs. What more could you ask for?

The sunrise had bathed the sky in honey and amber as Pete piloted his skiff into the back of Sail Bay. We were heading straight for a favorite drift along Santa Clara and Briarfield Coves. The area's lush grass beds are a haven for shrimp and tiny baitfish. It's a prolific food factory for hungry bass.

Our skiff was positioned so the drift would parallel the transition line between the sloping beach and the deeper grass cover. We worked our flies from the center of the green carpet radiating toward the shoreline edge. Crystal-clear water provided a view of every undulating blade of grass. In fact, we could watch our flies dart about and seduce the spotties into action. It was rare to make the drift without a positive response from a beautiful bass.

From grass beds and docks to open-water current lanes and the deep, swirling eddies of bridge pilings, all it takes is one outing to become addicted to fly fishing for spotted bass. If you live near or visit the central and southern parts of the Pacific coastline, why drive hours to the Sierra for trout when cooperative spotties are waiting to be caught practically on your own doorstep? Historically, sand bass ranged from the Santa Cruz/Monterey area down into Baja and even along Mexico's northwest-ern mainland, but overharvesting has diminished their range. Today, major concentrations in California occur from Ventura to San Diego. Spotted bass also are prime gamefish in many of the Baja peninsula's estuaries.

Spring sounds the starting gun for Southern California's saltwater

FLY PORTRAITS AND COLOR PHOTOS

Albion Flat estuary, Northern California.
PHOTOGRAPH BY GLENN KISHI

A typical central California slough.
PHOTOGRAPH BY GLENN KISHI

Baranof Wilderness Lodge, Warm Springs Bay, southeast Alaska.
PHOTOGRAPH BY GLENN KISHI

Clockwise from top left:
The author and Jay Murakoshi dressed for surf fishing, Monterey Bay, California.

Working a trough in Santa Cruz County, California.

Alaskan silver salmon, Chatham Strait, southeast Alaska.

Dusky rockfish, Takatz Bay, southeast Alaska.

Silver salmon release, Chatham Strait, southeast Alaska.

PHOTOGRAPHS BY GLENN KISHI

Clockwise from top left:
Blue shark tagged for study, Monterey Bay, California.
PHOTOGRAPH BY KEN HANLEY

Dan Blanton with a striped bass in San Francisco Bay
PHOTOGRAPH BY KEN HANLEY

Glenn Kishi with his first white seabass, Capitola Kelp Beds, California.
PHOTOGRAPH BY KEN HANLEY

Spotted sand bass, Mission Bay, San Diego, California.
PHOTOGRAPH BY GLENN KISHI

Clockwise from top left:
Pacific mackerel, Los Angeles Harbor.
PHOTOGRAPH BY GLENN KISHI

*Paul Yearance with skipjack tuna,
East Cape, Baja California, Mexico.*
PHOTOGRAPH BY KEN HANLEY

*Fine tuned tackle matches habitat
and species.*
PHOTOGRAPH BY GLENN KISHI

ALF Baitfish (created by Bill and Kate Howe)

CDC Shrimp (created by Michael Andersen)

Clouser Minnow (created by Bob Clouser)

Deep Candy Bendback (created by Bob Popovics)

Deer Hair Shrimp (created by Jack Horner)

Diamond Shrimp (created by Ken Hanley)

Fatal Attraction (created by Dan Blanton)

Flashtail Whistler (created by Dan Blanton)

Gold Buccaneer (created by Ken Hanley)

Green Comet

Jay's Grass Shrimp (created by Jay Murakoshi)

Jensen Foam Slider (created by Milt Jensen)

Labyrinth Crab (created by Ken Hanley)

Lefty's Deceiver (created by Lefty Kreh)

Micro Shrimp (created by Jay Murakoshi)

Near 'Nuff Sculpin (created by Dave Whitlock)

Pearl Yeti (created by Ken Hanley)

Pink Pollywog (created by Dec Hogan)

Rabbit-Strip Fly

Rusty Squirrel Clouser (variation of Bob Clouser's Minnow by Jay Murakoshi)

Salmon Waker (created by Larry Dahlberg)

Sea Arrow Squid (created by Dan Blanton)

Sea Habit Bucktail (created by Trey Combs)

Sockeye Boss (created by Rich Culver)

Sockeye Special

Sorcerer's Touch (created by Ken Hanley)

Surf Grub (created by Ken Hanley)

Surfpercher Red (created by John Shewey)

Tres Generation Popper (created by Dale Hightower)

Tropical Punch (created by Dan Blanton)

V-Worm (created by Andy Burk)

Sand bass comparison: spotted sand bass are covered with dark spots.
PHOTOGRAPH BY GLENN KISHI

Sand bass comparison: barred sand bass show heavy bars and drab color.
PHOTOGRAPH BY GLENN KISHI

bass derby. Anyone venturing into the protected harbors or inshore waters of the region can celebrate the arrival of sand bass in shallow water. These superb gamefish may seem to resemble their freshwater counterparts, but if you plan on lip-locking your catch for a picture, take heed. These briny bass have a full set of needle-sharp teeth.

Spotted sand bass (*Paralabrax maculatofasciatus*) are a handsome lot. Their bodies and fins are covered with a multitude of black spots. They're

The profile of the barred bass is similar to that of other bottom-oriented species.
PHOTOGRAPH BY GLENN KISHI

sort of the rainbow trout of the salty bass family. Spotties are brown or olive across the back, with the same colors fading as they get closer to the fish's belly. Subtle side barring is also present on most specimens. Barred sand bass (*Paralabrax nedulifer*), or "bars," as they're known, sport distinctive dark bars and blotches on their sides. The foundation color of the bars may vary from gray to olive.

Both of these species share a similar fin structure. Their long dorsals have prominent spines, the third spine being the tallest. Their caudal fins are broad-surfaced and square-cut, broomlike in appearance. Both their pectoral and their anal fins are broad-surfaced, as well. Sharp spines are present on the lead edge of the anal fin.

Spotted bass are generally twelve to twenty-two inches in length. One of the largest on record weighed five pounds, eight ounces. Barred bass are the larger species of the two, attaining a length of just over twenty-five inches. Would you believe an eleven-pound, one-ounce specimen is on record? It is!

Spots and bars can be found year-round. Typically, May is the kickoff month for the spawning cycle of sand bass, the month when they begin to head for shallower water. Schools moving into the shallows seem to prefer hard-bottomed habitat. Barred sand bass tend to be found more often over packed sand, while the spotted bass will be found over both sandy and mud bottoms.

Fly fishers can explore this fishery whether they're working from a boat or the bank. Anglers on foot can cast their flies along jetty walls, rocky outcroppings, and directly into the surf zone. Small-craft operators have the advantage of extreme mobility, including access to highly productive nearshore habitat.

If you'll be on foot, nighttime is probably the most productive period for taking bass from around built cover. Work your streamers on the calmer side of jetties and breakwaters, because that's where the sand bass congregate. The turbulence on the outer wall attracts a different variety of gamefish, such as surfperch and white seabass.

No matter how and where you prefer to track down these fish, the key to success is to fish currents, because the bass see them as food-delivery systems. Keep an eye open for eddies, current seams, and work the moving tide. Channel rips can be a highway for sand bass, too.

When it comes to tackle, the environment you'll be working in determines what you should choose. Outfits ranging from 7-weight through 9-weight can be right on target. Inside Southern California's protected harbors, the lighter rods will be fine. Once you begin working outside the surf line, however, you'll learn to appreciate the extra insurance of a heavier rod.

Line choice is straightforward: you need to get your offering down. Sinking shooting heads or integrated shooting heads and running lines are the ticket around here. You could find yourself fishing for bass anywhere from a few feet under the surface to well over forty feet deep. A full-sinking intermediate line and a fast-sinking shooting head rated at 200 grains or heavier are cornerstone choices for me.

My leader system is fairly long. I start with 6 or 7 feet of tapered leader and adjust my tippet length as required. I prefer to use tippet material rated at 10 or 12 pounds. The overall leader could be as long as 10 to 12 feet, if necessary. When I fish strong currents or turbulent waters, I shorten the leader to 5 or 6 feet overall.

Fly patterns should resemble the local baitfish, particularly anchovies. Streamers two to four inches in length are optimum. A silver body with blue back accent is a prime color scheme. Various options include silver and gray, silver and green, and all-white. Popular patterns include Clouser Minnows, small ALFs, and Deep Candy Bendbacks.

Another food item of note for sand bass is bay shrimp. Small Rabbit-Strip Flies in white, brown, or gray are perfect for imitating these crustaceans.

On the other hand entirely, hot-pink plastic lures are winners for conventional-tackle anglers. I couldn't stop thinking about that, so I began to experiment with Rabbit-Strip Flies that look like they came from the Energizer Bunny and enjoyed wildly successful days. Why does the pink work? I don't know, it just does, and that's good enough for me.

Fly fishers exploring the waters just outside the breaking surf can add squid imitations to their fly collections. A Sea Arrow Squid or a white Rabbit-Strip Fly can produce plenty of positive results. Boat anglers might establish a chum line, as well. Sandies definitely show a strong response to a well-defined feeding lane.

Kelp bass (*Paralabrax clathratus*), also known as calico bass, are another prize found around rocky shorelines and kelp forests from Southern California down to Baja. Sometimes confused with the yellowtail rockfish, calicos are actually members of the sea bass family, Serranidae. They resemble rockfish in body type, though, with a robust profile, large, broomlike tail, huge mouth, and big eyes. The fish's color scheme is predominantly olive and brown. Its sides are slightly mottled, giving way to a much lighter belly. One of the calico's distinguishing features is the presence of large, distinct, pale blotches across its back.

These bass spawn beginning in the late spring and continue into the early fall. Like their rockfish counterparts, they are slow to reach maturity. It takes them approximately four years to get to that stage in life. In order to protect the future of the species, California has regulated both bag and size limits. It's a smart move for managing this unique resource.

Putting together a collection of flies for this gamefish is easy. Squid and sardines are the preferred prey. Use hooks sized 2/0 or 4/0 for these imitations. Other baitfish and crustacean imitations can be productive, but are frequently the second choice of both fish and anglers. Still, it's to your benefit to carry a sampling of these patterns, just in case you need them. Dark days or dark waters also might require darker patterns.

Squid populations increase throughout the winter. Though many fly fishers prefer to fish in warmer conditions, the winter months are prime for targeting some of the largest bass of the year.

Look for kelp bass—surprise!—around kelp. A kelp forest with rock structure is ideal. This environment definitely will abuse your tackle, though, so come prepared to deal with sharp edges and tangles. You'll

Kelp Bass are a treasure from Southern California to Baja.
PHOTOGRAPH BY GLENN KISHI

need to apply instant pressure on the fish in order to free them from structure and cover. Appropriate tools for this adventure are 10-weight rods. Some fly fishers even prefer heavier rods for calico expeditions.

Sinking shooting heads provide exactly what you need in the line department. Carrying a couple with different sink rates lets you adjust your presentation based on variations in current strength, the ocean swell, the depth at which fish feed, and the density of the cover. A standard lead-core head plus a second shooting head of at least 400 grains should cover the entire water column. You could find these fish suspended from a few feet under the surface to well below sixty feet.

Keep in mind the strength and size of the species. You need to keep your rod tip low, strip strike with authority, and lean into the butt of your rod while pulling the fish out of cover. Forget about playing them off the reel—keep the pressure on while you hand strip to control your line. It's a quick contest, usually won or lost within seconds of the bite.

Calicos will surge into any sanctuary they can find when hooked. Your line could be driven into a maze of crevices. It could be wound around the holdfast or thick stipes of giant perennial kelp. If you happen to be unfortunate enough to have this happen, take heart. There's a technique that could swing the odds back in your favor. If you've exerted maximum pressure and there appears to be a standoff, just back off. Ease the pressure you've applied on the bass. In fact, remove enough pressure to create a semislack line. When you allow the natural rhythms of the sea to take over, the bass may start to move once again, often abandoning the shelter it sought and clearing your line. This technique is often employed on commercial party boats fishing for rockfish, lingcod, halibut, and other bottom dwellers.

If you're having a tough time finding productive calico habitat, here's another tip. Small-craft operators should look for lobster or crab pot sets. The traps are a great indicator of rock piles, pinnacles, and other significant structure. Anytime I come across lobster or crab pots, I know I have a shot at some terrific action. Those traps attract more than crustaceans to the area.

With all this talk about working tight to cover and structure, tide choice becomes critical. Most anglers agree that prime time occurs around high tide. On days with big tidal swings, fish the last two hours of the incoming tide through the first two hours of the outgoing tide. Better yet, choose a neap tide. Its smaller fluctuation between high and low tides probably will produce an extended bite. The idea is to look for conditions that flood prime habitat and minimize extreme fluctuations around cover. You do need to be in an area that provides some current, though, because this enhances movement of bait within the region.

Crab pots are prime beacons for drawing gamefish.
PHOTOGRAPH BY KEN HANLEY

Never pass up the opportunity to explore the environment of pots and traps.
PHOTOGRAPH BY KEN HANLEY

Glenn Kishi with his first white seabass.
PHOTOGRAPH BY KEN HANLEY

I THINK I'M BECOMING A fatalist. Sometimes, it seems like what will be, will be, regardless of anything we try to do about it. We all know individuals who've busted a gut trying to achieve something that just seems to come unsought to someone else who was at the right place at the right time. That's the story behind Bill Matthews's first white seabass.

Bill and Cary Asper headed their skiff straight for Horseshoe Kelp. This area is a highly productive fishery located approximately four miles off Long Beach, California. Conditions were perfect for making the run: a minimal swell, low winds, and an ocean surface as flat as a billiard table. It was the fastest trip either of them had ever experienced to "The Shoe."

Horseshoe Kelp lies in fairly deep water. The kelp forest is anchored near the twenty-fathom mark—120 feet. The location is noted for the outstanding opportunities it offers for connecting with California barracudas, calico bass, rockfish, Pacific mackerel, jack mackerel, and bonito. Although white seabass are caught in the area, they're more likely to be found in the nearshore habitat of Sunset Beach or northward around Point Vicente and up along the kelp line of Malibu Beach.

Cary piloted the skiff into position along a prominent current seam. Bill had set up a 10/11-weight outfit rigged with a Teeny TS 450 sinking line. His 7-foot leader was tapered down to a 12-pound tippet, with a green-and-white 2/0 Deceiver knotted to the end. As Cary kept an eye on the drift, Bill made his first cast of the day. On his third sharp strip—WHAM—the fly was ambushed by something hefty. Bill's fish had struck the streamer at about twenty-five feet deep. Neither he nor Cary knew what had eaten the fly yet.

The water conditions were clear enough for Bill to see the fish swirl. It was a deep bronze. Perhaps a thresher shark? The brown, bronze, and gold threshers are common enough in the area. The fish immediately dove toward the kelp forest's tangles and structure, and Bill struggled with it for over thirty minutes before gaining some ground. In the meantime, Cary was yelling and coaching like a maniac.

Bill finally was able to get the fish swimming back toward the surface, and that's when they got their first eye-to-eye look at it. Cary's reaction— "It's a bleeping seabass!!!"—was the beginning of an amazing flurry of bleeps that pounded against Bill's eardrums. There was no denying the creature was huge. With all the excitement, the guys had worked themselves into a feverish state. Cary got the net, Bill began working the fish boatside, and of course Cary missed his first pass with the net.

When the prize finally was brought under control and brought aboard the skiff, Cary thought there was a chance the bass was a record catch, and boy, was he ever right. Bill Matthews's white seabass, weighing a total of seventeen pounds, eight ounces, and measuring forty-three inches, was accepted as a new world record for the 16-pound class tippet. Did I mention it was his first cast of the day? And that it was Bill's first white seabass? Breaking records was the farthest thing from their mind. They were going for barracuda. But Bill was in the right place, at the right time. Now tell me fate had nothing to do with that!

The white seabass (*Atractoscion nobilis*) is the largest member of the croaker family, the only species in the family capable of attaining weights greater than twenty pounds. Its elongated body makes it somewhat resemble a striped bass in shape. The fin structure is broad-surfaced, and the long dorsal is deeply notched, with the forward portion supported by a series of stiff spines. The bass's fins are perfectly adapted to living around kelp in heavy currents.

Young fish are typically silver overall, with a slight tinge of copper-colored vertical barring on the side. Their fins are often a dusky yellow. Adult seabass, however, are predominantly a rich bronze or copper on the back, with some specimens developing a steel-gray appearance, instead. Speckling across the back also is present on most specimens. The bass's sides are silver, quickly fading into a white belly.

White seabass begin to spawn in the late spring and continue throughout the summer months. Nursery waters are often in shallow environments such as estuaries, protected bays, and calm, sandy beaches. The shelter of the kelp forest is an area where you'll find both young and mature fish. They are typically a schooling species. Adults also will concentrate their movements around deep, rocky bottom cover and within the surf zone itself.

Historically, these bass were known to roam the entire Pacific coastline, from southeast Alaska to southern Baja. Today, however, the species is confined to the warmer waters of the Southland. The once-thriving populations of wild white seabass are now augmented by hatchery-grown specimens. This hatchery program was the result of a personal initiative undertaken by Milt Shedd, the founder of Hubbs–Sea World Research Institute. Concerned about the future of his local fisheries, Milt assembled a team of scientists and fisheries specialists to identify a species most likely to respond favorably to a controlled rearing environment. The white seabass was chosen as a result of this multiyear search. As part of the implementation of the program necessary to preserve and enhance this fishery, California removed the bass from commercial harvest and adopted both size and bag limits for the sport angling community.

The Hubbs–Sea World Research Institute and the California Marine Hatchery Institute are responsible for the harvest of broodstock and initial steps in raising the fry. Once the juveniles reach a length of three inches, they're transferred to rearing pens at twelve facilities throughout Southern California. Developing this large-scale rearing program and implementing the widespread distribution of the stock has led to a highly successful conservation effort. Today, you can target them from California down into Baja as far as Magdalena Bay. The areas most frequently productive for flyrodders include the San Diego region (Point Loma Kelp, Silver Strand Beach, La Jolla), the Los Angeles area (Newport Bay, Sunset Beach, Horseshoe Kelp, Point Vicente, Malibu Beach), around Santa Barbara (The Harbor, Carpenteria), and, increasingly, around Monterey Bay's Capitola kelp beds.

The bass will eat sardines and mackerel, but squid or anchovies are what they prefer. Fly patterns should include Clousers, Deceivers, and certainly some Sea Arrow Squids. Hook sizes should vary from 1/0 to 4/0. Color schemes of silver, green and white, blue and white, and dark blue and green will cover the entire spectrum well. Baitfish imitations of four to six inches in length are appropriate choices on most outings. If you have the skill and confidence to throw a bigger fly, then by all means give it a go. It's well known that on certain days the bass will key only on larger mackerel.

You need the backbone of a 10-weight or 11-weight rod to redirect these gamefish away from kelp tangles and sharp-edged rocks. Don't underestimate the bulldogging strength of these bass. Integrated shooting heads and running lines with a weight of 400 to more than 500 grains or traditional Type 4, Type 6, and LC-13 lead-core shooting heads will sink your flies to the proper feeding levels. Most of your fishing will be done in the depth range of fifteen to twenty-five feet.

Leader and tippet combinations should be pretty stout. Again, 7-foot leaders seem to be the most popular. Be sure the butt section is robust enough to turn over heavy and bulky flies. A classic example would use a 30-pound butt section coupled to a 20-pound tippet. You could always go lighter on the tippet if you feel it's necessary for the presentation. Since the fish have a set of teeth located in the roofs of their mouths, you might consider adding a short bite trace, if you do use a lighter tippet.

Boaters will no doubt have the best access to prime white-seabass habitat, but if you're a shore angler, don't let that statement discourage you from exploring this fishery. Fishing along breakwaters, sandy flats adjacent to deep channels, and in the surf zone pays big dividends for walking fly fishers every year. The seabass encountered in harbors and estuaries are likely to be juveniles and young adults averaging less than five pounds. The majority of the fly-rod fish caught in deeper water off reefs and around kelp beds, however, will average seven to ten pounds.

Peter Piconi celebrates with a California barracuda.
PHOTOGRAPH BY GLENN KISHI

AT FIRST, IT WAS JUST A FEW sparkles suspended in the current. They were the scales of baitfish. Fifteen minutes later, there were a lot, filtering our way, along with some dollops of fish oil welling to the surface. Something was feeding just above our drift. It was enough to make us reposition the boat. Still, there was no skipping bait, and there were no explosions of predators on the surface. Whatever was causing the carnage, it must have been going on pretty deep.

Then, across the channel, we witnessed a frantic flurry of gulls and terns. That was the sign we wanted. Arriving on the scene, we immediately caught glimpses of flashes near the boat: barracudas. After slashing through the baitfish down below, they now were in a feeding frenzy at the surface, shooting like silver tracers through the clouds of anchovies.

Can you think of a faster gamefish for its size? Ounce for ounce and inch for inch, the California barracuda is one heck of a sleek feeding machine. Locals have a number of names they use to describe the species: "barries," "scooters," "snakes," "stove pipes," "slimers," and, for the larger specimens, "logs." No matter what the size, I like to refer to them as "vipers." Their strike is like a cobra's, lightening-quick. Heaven forbid you should experience one at boatside. It's enough to stand up the hair on the back of your neck.

The California barracuda (*Sphyraena argentea*) is extremely long for its width and height. Its fins are small, fairly stiff, and well spaced. They add little in the way of drag, yet maximize the creature's ability to maneuver at high speeds. The barracuda's back is a combination of brown, blue, and gray. The sides are a brilliant silver, sometimes fading into a slightly white belly. A handsome black lateral line accents the flank. Occasionally, you'll discover an individual that sports faint barring just above the lateral mark. Another distinct coloration is the dusky yellow tail fin. The fin itself is forked, once again adapted for high-speed travel.

The trademark of a 'cuda is of course its needle-sharp teeth. You might be surprised by their size, though. They're quite large. The 'cuda also is equipped with a strong set of elongated jaws to help it take care of business. Think of baitfish first and foremost when you consider tying imitations for the barrie's diet. Anchovies, herring, smelt, sardines, and even squid are the target fare.

Pacific barracudas are smaller than the Atlantic version. The majority of sport-caught fish range from two to four feet in length. Their weight is typically under five pounds. Plenty of larger specimens of seven pounds or more are caught every year, though. It's widely accepted by biologists, that any California barracuda nearing the ten-pound range is most likely a female. There's also an eighteen-pound specimen on record.

The barracuda's spawning cycle begins in the early spring and continues throughout the summer, with fish spawning as early as two years old. The spawn takes place in the open ocean. It's likely the waters off the Baja peninsula are the preferred location. The eggs are pelagic and drift with the currents. As the young develop, they seek shelter in more protected environments, such as harbors, estuaries, and calmer nearshore waters. Unlike the rockfish, the barracuda is a fairly rapidly growing species.

Historically, these gamefish roamed the Pacific coastline from the cold waters off Kodiak Island down into the warm waters off southern Baja. Barracuda now have a more limited range, most likely as a result of natural causes such as fluctuations in ocean temperatures. Today, you'll find the majority in waters south of Point Conception in California, on down along the Baja peninsula. You can find barracudas year-round off the Baja coast. Massive schools roam the coastline in a seasonal fashion, following preferred water temperatures and baitfish populations. Their northern migration is in full swing during the summer, and that's when Southern California's barracuda fishery thrives. Barracudas tend to travel back toward the southern reaches of their range during the late autumn and winter. However, in recent years, the California fishery has a growing population of 'cuda that have evolved into year-round residents, probably because of changes in water temperatures brought about by El Niño.

Barries frequent nearshore open waters, kelp beds, estuaries, and harbors. They're a surface-oriented species. It's uncommon to come across them traveling at depths of more than sixty feet. You're more likely to find schools of barracudas ripping through bait balls in water ten to fifteen feet deep. You'll even see them busting bait at the surface.

My favorite rod for this type of angling is an 8-weight. It provides plenty of backbone, yet it's light enough to cast all day. Outfits ranging in size from 7-weights to 10-weights are commonly used, though. The tranquil waters inside a harbor provide the perfect conditions for a light outfit. Chasing 'cuda along the open coast could require an upgrade to heavier tackle, and usually does.

Integrated shooting heads and running lines are the lines of choice. If you carry only one line, make it a superfast-sinking model. A standard Type 6 shooting head, or one made from LC-13, are other possibilities. The heavier heads let you present the fly as deep as necessary. By starting your retrieve as the fly hits the water, you'll be able to use the same lines to work just a few feet under the surface effectively, as well.

Should you use leaders with steel bite traces, or mono? That's an ongoing dilemma. Stiff wire leaders could hinder the action of your fly during a retrieve. Some folks also believe the fish get spooked by a wire trace. I haven't experienced that. Still, I usually use mono. I use a 3-foot butt section of 35-pound test coupled to a 2-foot tippet rated at 14 pounds. I finish the system with a short, foot-long bite trace, typically one rated at 20 pounds. I feel the lighter tippet helps to impart more action during my presentation. I also believe the elasticity of the tippet helps absorb any sudden impact. Overall, the leader is 6 to 9 feet in length. I simply adjust the tippet length if I find the fish to be a bit spooky. Another popular setup is to use a factory-made tapered leader rated at 12 or 14 pounds and add a short bite trace. If you want to make life simpler yet, just use a straight 7-foot piece of 20-pound mono. Many of the fly fishers I've run into do.

Though I favor mono, I've found some of the newer wire designs to be pretty productive. The most flexible I've come across are produced by the American Fishing Wire company. Their Surflonr-Micro, which is made of nylon-coated stainless steel, is a fine product.

Nobody can look at a barracuda's teeth and not think "Baitfish," and indeed, baitfish and squid are their primary food items. Your flies should resemble anchovies, in particular. A silver body with a chartreuse or olive back accent is a premiere color scheme. Streamers two to four inches long are ideal. Additional flies representing baby squid, sardines, herring, or smelt can round out the collection. Color options might include silver and gray, silver and blue, and all-white. Clouser Minnows, small ALFs, and Deep Candy Bendbacks are top-producing patterns. Sizes vary from 2 to 3/0. Fly patterns that are constructed to incorporate a jigging-style motion have a distinct advantage.

Considering the fish's toothy nature, you'd best be served by carrying a large number of flies. Even the best-constructed get ripped up during a 'cuda session. Don't forget to check the integrity of your leader and tippet material frequently, as well. Nicks and abrasions could cost you a fly and a fish or two.

There are a few schools of thought about what I call puppeteering your fly—animating it during the retrieve to resemble a baitfish whose actions say "Dinner is served" to a predator. One favors imitating fleeing, fast-moving prey. I generally use this approach when I'm working my fly close to the surface. You can accomplish a speedy retrieve by using a long, single-handed pull or a somewhat shorter pull as part of a double-overhand technique, with your rod tucked under your arm. I like the puppeteering effect of longer pulls that incorporate a slight pause in between the action. This zip-dip-zip-dip rhythm is terrific for mimicking injured prey. If you prefer to work with the double-overhand retrieve, be sure to allow the fly to pause every so often. This change of movement, a downward flutter, is often the trigger that brings a strike. Another approach is to yo-yo the fly. Let your line sink fairly deep, then begin with a long pull, followed by a very long pause. The idea is to exaggerate the action of the fly. 'Cuda frequently hit injured bait on the drop.

Paul Yearance and prize skipjack tuna.
PHOTOGRAPH BY KEN HANLEY

PAUL YEARANCE AND ERIC SUMTER had never caught a fly-rod tuna. In fact, neither one had ever caught a tuna at all. Like most of us, they got their tuna from cans. I was conducting a week-long clinic on inshore tactics, though, with a curriculum that included rocky shorelines, shallow bays and reefs, and the sandy-bottomed surf zone. That day's lesson dealt with snappers and small tuna.

We'd discussed tackle options prior to heading out, and on the water we reviewed the natural history of the fish, knot applications and terminal rigging, boating tactics, fly presentations, and playing the fish. We then ran the boat parallel to the shoreline no more than a mile off the beaches and rocky cover. Following major current lanes and noting any color breaks, we scanned the area for feeding activity: diving birds, skipping bait, boils and "nervous water," and perhaps a rocketing tuna or two. In addition, any dark water could be an indication of baitfish being herded to the surface by predators from below. Scanning is one of those skills that can be developed only on the water. It takes a keen eye to eliminate unproductive waters and increase your chances of fishing over feeding fish. Working as a team, we were able to spot feeding fish fairly regularly.

In a skiff a mile out in the Pacific, on a rocking platform and casting to fast-moving targets, you need to be versatile in your casting techniques. Standard overhead casts rarely are employed. It's a whole new world for those accustomed to the relatively stable conditions experienced while wading estuary flats.

The basic technique, Paul and Eric had learned, was the "quick stroke." It entails having some running line coiled at your feet and at least half of a shooting head draped off the rod while you hold the hook and leader in a ready position to create a quick flip and continue into a single backstroke to shoot some line. Once they had the quick stroke under control, they could build on it by using sidearm casts and reverse casts, actually presenting the fly on the back stroke. With the line in the water, water hauling, using the friction of the shooting head in the water to load the rod, would prove another essential technique for quick, efficient presentations. Ambidextrous casters have a definite advantage on these adventures because they can present their flies from either side of the boat without spiffing up their companions with pierced-ear pendants of fur and feathers.

In order to avoid that kind of confusion or worse, we established a rotation of anglers in the casting station. The idea was to allow each fly fisher in turn a maximum of presentation time during a single pass over active fish. This included allowing multiple casts if the need arose. The casting station was in the stern of the craft, which allowed for freedom to pilot the boat and prepare the angler's presentation. While one angler was in the "batter's box," the fly fisher waiting in the "on deck" position acted as spotter and cleared the fly line of any obstructions during the fighting and handling of a catch. A third angler was in control of camera gear and keeping track of the schooling tuna.

We'd spotted nervous water and were heading on an intercept course for a massive school of skipjack tuna slashing away at prey. The school

Surface-running tuna feasting on baitfish.
PHOTOGRAPH BY KEN HANLEY

stretched for at least a hundred yards. There must have been hundreds upon hundreds of tuna on the move. It's an awesome sight to behold.

Paul was first up. He made a cast directly into the melee of feeding fish, but completed his retrieve without getting a hit. I suggested he place his second cast more along the edge of the school. Instantly, a tuna cut from the pack. He saw the fish flash and felt a jarring hit. The ensuing conversation went something like this:

Paul: "Its taking line! What do I do!"

Ken: "Cool—let it run a while."

Paul: "No, I mean it's really *taking line*. What do I *do*!!"

Ken: "Cool—let it run a while, you probably couldn't stop it anyway. Building up some line drag is a good thing."

I instructed Paul to take a deep breath and stay calm. Sometimes that's easier said than done. He smiled, then dug in his heels and prepared to learn about line drag, palming his spool, and playing the angles against the fish. Whenever he was able to detect a slight pause or weakening in the tuna's run, he used the rod as leverage and quickly regained some line, then immediately exerted pressure from a different angle to keep the fish working against the gear. It took him twenty minutes to bring the fish to hand.

In the meantime, the school had regrouped a short distance away. By the time we arrived near it again, it was running deeper, but only ten to fifteen feet under the surface. Eric was up next. He made his presentation and waited for the line to drop into "the zone." We could see numerous fish working below the fly. He began his retrieve with a long, sharp pull, and instantly the fly was mugged. His fish shot straight down, driving the rod tip into the water. The reel was screaming, and Eric began to apply steady pressure by palming the rim. He could sense the fish was tiring from the dive. He'd soon have hands-on experience learning to "pump" a tuna, a technique that requires a short lifting stroke (ideally keeping the rod tip no higher than his waist) and then quickly reeling down to regain line as the rod is lowered under control. A rapid series of short pumps is best. After some serious give-and-take, Eric applied pressure from various side angles once the fish had been brought back toward the surface. It wasn't long before Eric was holding his first tuna. His hands were still shaking. He'd become a full-fledged member of the "Skippie Club."

Tuna have that wonderful football-shaped body. These gamefish are solid, thick-muscled creatures, buff hardbodies that get that way because they have to keep moving to breathe. They have a negative buoyancy and no ability to hover. If they stop moving, they die. That's a real motive for aerobic exercise. Their shape is fine-tuned to reduce drag and maximize momentum. Black skipjack tuna (*Euthynnus lineatus*) reduce some of the drag by not being fully scaled. Scales exist as a "corselet" located only around the head and the forward third of the body. Other friction-reducing features include a retractable first dorsal fin that fits into a slot and eyes that lie flat against the head and are covered by an adipose eyelid. A pointed snout, stiff, small-surfaced fins, a short, thin tail stock and extremely forked tail all contribute to the efficiency of each movement. The tuna's quick-beating tail rhythm is a signature of the species. Take another close look at the fish and you'll notice a series of small "finlets" behind both the dorsal and anal fins. Examining the base of the tail will also reveal a set of "keels." Combined, these features afford the tuna great stability in high-speed maneuvering. The finlets help to reduce turbulence along the tail section, while the keels assist in funneling water directly to the tail fin. The tail section is flat, rather than round in cross section, minimizing lateral resistance.

The iridescence of the black skipjack around the head and back is like an artist's palette, with various hues of blue, green, and purple. Its sides are predominantly mother-of-pearl white. Longitudinal rows of black stripes along the back often continue down to the belly, though the lower stripes may appear faded in many specimens. Large black spots are a typical marking found in the pectoral region.

Skippies are typically two to three feet in length and weigh under twelve pounds. Individual specimens can, and do, get bigger, however. They may be small, as tuna go, but you'd never suspect it from the brute strength they display at the end of your line.

This species is epipelagic—it prefers traveling in coastal waters. For fly fishers, that means they travel in water shallow enough to be caught on the long rod. Their range is from central California down through Central and South America. You can often encounter them schooling within a mile or so of the shoreline. Spawning takes place during the summer in Mexico's waters or farther south.

Skipjack tuna eat various baitfish, squid, and, to a lesser degree crustaceans. That means your fly collection can be pretty basic for skippies. Sea Habits, ALFs, Sea Arrow Squids, and a few Tres Generation poppers will offer you enough variety to stay with a hot bite. Just be sure your pattern selection includes baitfish imitations ranging from three to five inches long tied on hooks from 1/0 to 3/0.

Skipjacks will test your strength and endurance and the strength and endurance of your tackle. You'll want a 10-weight rod with either an integrated shooting head and running line or a traditional shooting head, rated from 300 to 400 or more grains. These heavier lines enable fine presentations at depths of five to fifteen feet. I also use an intermediate line for popper presentations. It helps to anchor the line below surface chop and turmoil. It also makes possible an outstanding combination retrieve rarely overlooked by hungry tuna, letting you pop the fly a few times on the surface to get a fish's attention, then puppeteer the fly to make it imitate the action of a crippled baitfish below the surface. Leaders with 12-pound tippets seem the norm. I know of a few seasoned pros who won't hesitate to drop down to eight-pound tippets to finesse a presentation if necessary, but I feel most confident with 12-pound or 16-pound material. These fish have teeth that can cut through tippets. You also could get "finned"—leaders have been abraded or cut by slashing tuna. If necessary, I add a short bite trace of 20-pound material if the tuna are particularly big and aggressive.

There's another great gamefish that has a body much like a skippie's and the power to match, the Pacific bonito (*Sarda chiliensis lineolata*). Unlike the black skipjack, with its instant, bulldogging dive, the bonito rips off scorching surface runs at first. But if you don't jump on a bonito right away, your hookup can turn into a deepwater tug-of-war as well. The bonito is slightly more elongated and therefore even more streamlined and less robust around the "shoulders" than the skipjack. The bonito isn't a true tuna, but shares a common family. The fin structure is similar, including finlets, a forked tail, and small-surfaced fins. Its two dorsals appear as one, the actual separation is so narrow. Unlike the skipjack, the Pacific bonito is fully scaled.

The most distinct markings on the bonito are the dark, oblique stripes along the back. They begin just in front of the lead dorsal fin and continue onto the wrist of the tail. The stripes vary in length and often extend slightly below the fish's lateral line. The bonito's back is a greenish blue, giving way to metallic silver on the sides and belly.

There are two recognized populations of Pacific bonito subspecies. The northern fish, which historically ranged from Alaska to the Baja peninsula are now found primarily around California to central Baja. The southern fish are concentrated around Peru and Chile. Part of the northern population spawns in Southern California in the winter and early spring. Both subspecies successfully spawn in waters much farther south each year.

*The author and Captain
Piconi show off a beauti-
fully marked Pacific
bonito.*
PHOTOGRAPH BY JEFF SOLIS

They favor coastal waters, including bays, rocky points, islands, and harbor habitats. Though bonito schools are frequently encountered in open bay environments, you could also find them traveling around kelp, along jetties, and roaming sandy shoals. When these gamefish enter harbors, they can be easily accessible to fly fishers on foot or in small craft.

The bonito's preferred diet consists of smaller baitfish such as sardines and anchovies two to four inches in length. Pinhead anchovies are a key food resource. Clouser Minnows, Deep Candy Bendbacks, Pearl Yetis, and small ALFs are terrific imitations tied on hooks from size 1 through 4. The bonito also target squid at times, particularly when the young are available. All-white Deceivers or smaller squid patterns imitate these menu choices well.

Rod and line requirements for bonito fishing mirror those for chasing the black skipjack. You can work with a lighter rod, an 8-weight or 9-weight, but don't discount a 10-weight's ability to put the hammer down when you need to control a fish. Tippets of 12-pound material are perfect for this game. Keep your leader short and simple—it needn't be longer than 5 feet. I know plenty of successful anglers who use 3-foot tippets.

PART 3
TACKLE AND TACTICS

SALTWATER FLY FISHING HAS BEEN around, in one form or another, for longer than you might imagine. Anglers have been fishing the salt with fly rods as far back as 1875, according to Genio Scott, author of *Fishing in American Waters,* who documents fly fishing for striped bass in New England. As a result, you'd think the design of salty gear would have been well established many moons ago. But in fact, rods, reels, lines, and other gear developed specifically for saltwater applications are fairly recent innovations. Today's designs, though, are proven winners that have been put to the test under some of the most extreme conditions you could imagine.

A variety of rods and reels allows you to explore all aspects of inshore fishing.
PHOTOGRAPH BY GLENN KISHI

The pioneers of saltwater fly fishing prior to the 1950s used freshwater rods because that was pretty much all there was. Experimentation in the salt continued, but the saltwater fly rod revolution didn't really get going until 1989, when Sage developed its RPLX design. Today, all the major rod companies and some of the upstarts have developed outstanding saltwater designs and continue to refine and extend their capabilities. At the same time, manufacturers have developed reels capable of withstanding the rigors of the salt, from the sand and spray of the surf zone to the big fish of blue water. Drag systems have become more efficient. Fly lines have been developed for a variety of specific saltwater applications and specific environments. The lines also cast farther, handle easier, and last longer. Tippets and leaders are more abrasion-resistant and harder for the fish to see. New hook designs are providing better holding power . . . and the list goes on. From tying materials to clothing and ancillary equipment, saltwater gear is now fully up to the task set by any Pacific saltwater adventure.

The evolution of this equipment is directly tied to the way anglers have been pushing the envelope, expanding saltwater fly fishing into new, unexplored areas and doing wild and wonderful new things. Because of this innovative spirit, fly-tackle designers have developed new and better products to meet changing demands, a process that will be certain to continue as more fly fishers come to the challenges of fishing in the salt. Let's take a closer look at the current state of the art.

RODS

The demands placed on saltwater rods include quick presentations, longer casts, handling heavy or bulky fly patterns, maximum leveraging and lifting power, and resistance to salt corrosion. Designers address these criteria by tinkering with everything from the chemistry of resins and fiber selection to experimenting with wall thickness and designing aggressive blank tapers. Oversized guides and tip tops are standard features for handling different fly lines or rigging schemes. Double-ring, uplocking reel seats are the choice of virtually all the leading manufacturers. Anodized aluminum, hard-chrome stainless steel, and titanium carbide are incorporated in various hardware and component designs. The complete rod is a high-tech wonder destined for extreme encounters.

With stronger and lighter materials used in the construction process, rods are lighter and easier to cast all day long. In addition to using the newer generations of graphite fiber, many manufacturers are turning to composite rod layups, also using other fibers such as fiberglass and Kevlar.

Freshwater anglers select their tackle according to the size of the gamefish they plan to pursue: light rods for small fish, heavy rods for big ones. In the salt, however, you play by the Pacific's rules. The conditions you'll face, not the size of the fish you expect to catch, dictate the rods and lines you need to use. Surfperch look like they'd be fun on 2-weight and 3-weight outfits, but try to cast those rods in a 15-knot wind or rescue your fly from a 300-pound mat of kelp washing in the surf zone and you'll know why you need something stouter. You might expect to use the same ultralight outfits to catch Pacific mackerel, but the rods won't provide the backbone to cast into tough winds or control the fish in heavy currents. The winds, waves, current speeds and intensities, depths, and types of cover you'll routinely encounter when fishing, along with the large, bulky baitfish imitations and the way that hooked fish can use those conditions to their advantage all are more important than the actual size and weight of a particular gamefish in determining what kind of gear you must use. The saltwater realm is inherently a tough place to catch a small fish, and even tougher place to land a large, aggressive predator. Take a practical approach and don't underestimate the potential demands put upon your fly rod. Also be aware that if you prefer to work with lighter rods, it's likely you'll discover a limited range of saltwater lines available to match the outfit. And unless the rod is custom made, the guides and hardware are probably freshwater designs not well suited for the techniques that saltwater fishing requires.

The lightest rods that you consistently can use in the salt are 6-weights and 7-weights. These rods excel when fishing shallow habitats and in calm conditions. Rod manufacturers, however, are constantly pushing the design envelope, and they have begun to come up with 5-weight rods designed specifically for saltwater applications, not for trout streams, so keep an eye on the market if you're a light-tackle enthusiast.

I'm confident using 6-weight and 7-weight rods for most gamefish up to five pounds. They're wonderful choices for chasing sand bass, barracudas, and smaller salmon, especially pinks, in estuaries, and 7-weights also are appropriate in mild surf conditions while targeting gamefish such as surfperch. The rigors of heavier surf require 8-weight rods, as do the waters of estuaries and relatively calm open seas. They're fine for surfperch, salmon up to ten pounds, mackerel, shallow rockfish, barracudas, and estuary flatfish. Difficult environmental conditions call for 9-weights and 10-weights. They'll also handle the toughest of gamefish covered in this book and are especially appropriate for kelp bass, large salmon, striped bass, white seabass, tuna, and sharks. You can count on these rods for fishing in rough surf conditions, around kelp beds, in swift currents, and in heavy winds. These rods also are terrific choices for deepwater applications. The 9-weights and 10-weights have tremendous lifting and leveraging power. They'll provide you with the ability to engage gamefish well beyond twenty pounds. Personally, I don't own anything heavier than a 10-weight outfit. I've handled blue sharks with this rod. If you feel more confident with a heavier rod, though, by all means go for it.

Today's salty fly fisher has a variety of choices in rod length, typically from 8 1/2 to 10 feet. Will you be fishing on foot? Are you wading deep, or working in heavy surf? Will you be casting from a boat? Are you often required to deliver quick, short-range presentations? Casting from kayaks, or while wading deep, or when facing high waves, or with a rising beach terrace or jetty behind you demands high backcasts that require longer rods. Conversely, if you're casting from skiffs, or in confined environments, or over fast-moving fish, shorter casting strokes and quicker deliveries are possible with shorter rods. If you want to try to fish the salt with ultralight outfits, 5-weights or lighter, though, longer rods will absorb any sudden shock while controlling and landing your catch.

REELS

Even though you most likely won't be doing much of your fishing on a long-range bluewater expedition, you're still going to need a reel you can count on to hold up under the rigors of the saltwater environment and the punishment dealt out by the fish that live there. It should be tough, smooth-running, possess a relatively large drag surface, and handle a variety of line and rigging combinations.

Well-crafted saltwater reels typically feature anodized protection. This process not only provides resistance to saltwater corrosion, but creates a tough, abrasion-resistant outer coating, as well. The anodizing process is particularly effective on reels that are machined from bar-stock aluminum. Die-cast reels require an alternate process to protect the metal. Coats of urethane, powder-coat paint, or other substances are applied over the surface to cover the metal parts. "Coated" protection provides less abrasion resistance, and a breach in the coating generally leads to corrosion all too soon.

Saltwater gamefish pull hard. They're capable of blistering runs. Drag systems on reels need to provide consistent pressure. If you're chasing large gamefish, the drag must be able to withstand sustained battles. Most saltwater drags work by compressing a metal plate against a softer disk. The larger the surface area, the better. Cork has been the disk material of choice for decades. It's still a favorite with many of the top manufacturers. Low start-up inertia and good heat dissipation are two key characteristics of cork. Other high-grade materials such as Delrin, Teflon, and Rulon are composites found in premium drag designs.

Having the ability to make quick and easy drag adjustments is a real plus, but to be completely in control fighting a gamefish, look for reels with an exposed rim that allows you to palm the spool. Using the palm of your hand against the rim to add and modulate extra friction makes possible an almost unlimited range of rapid responses during a fight.

The gamefish you choose to target will dictate your backing needs, but be sure your reel has the capacity to store at least 75 yards of backing. If you plan on pursuing seabass and skipjacks, for example, you'd be wise to have a reel that provides 150 yards or more.

Large-arbor reels eliminate tight coiling that could hinder casting distance or interfere with carrying on a fight. The design also protects tippets from undue pressure as the fly line and backing leave the reel. The difference in circumference between a full reel spool and one with its backing rapidly disappearing into the briny deep is less. On a conventional reel, as the backing runs out and the effective circumference of the spool rapidly diminishes, there's less leverage for the fish to use as it pulls against the drag, and the resistance applied to the fish and tippet therefore increases without the drag setting being increased. With a large-arbor reel, the circumference doesn't change as much when the spool empties, and the amount of effective drag therefore stays closer to the amount you set to protect your tippet. Large-arbor designs also retrieve more line per turn of the spool than conventional reels.

Fly Lines

Fly lines lend themselves to experimentation, and manufacturers constantly are experimenting with them. I'm as ready as anyone to try out the results, but Pacific inshore fly fishers would do well to begin with the basics: sink-tip lines, intermediate lines, and sinking shooting heads or integrated shooting heads and running lines. Don't get overwhelmed with the choices available. You'll do fine starting with just two or three lines in your kit.

I have one line for most of the fishing I do on or near the surface, plus a changeable shooting-head setup with one head for middle depths and moderate currents and another for deep water and strong currents. In this way, using just two spools, you can cover everything from shallow grassy flats to deeper reefs. Even though I own more lines, I find myself gravitating to this simplified setup.

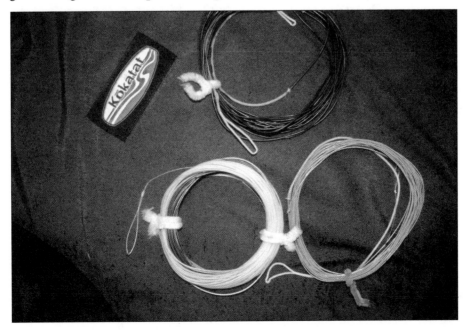

Sinking lines bring action in the Pacific fisheries.
Photograph by Ken Hanley

A full line with an intermediate sink rate is my choice for surface-oriented presentations in places like shallow flats and calm estuary interiors, even if I'm working with poppers or sliders. I also use it for subsurface streamers around kelp beds and in open-water environments. The intermediate line has a small diameter and casts beautifully. I recommend seeking out a model that's clear or translucent for stealthy presentations.

If you prefer to cast full lines, rather than shooting heads, integrated shooting head and running line systems are fine options for mid- to deep-water presentations. You'll have no problem negotiating moderate or heavy current flows with these lines, either. They're a shooting head that's permanently spliced to a smaller diameter running line. The heads are typically 24 to 30 feet in length and come in a wide variety of grain weights. Currently, the lightest is rated at 130 grains, while the heaviest is more than 700. If you own only one of these lines, try to make it a 250-grain or 350-grain model for versatility. Of course, if you fish extreme depths or extreme current flows, you could need a heavier line. Your rod will actually dictate the range of grain weights that are optimal for loading the blank.

There's a long tradition among Pacific Coast fly fishers of fishing with sophisticated shooting-head systems. They originally were developed in the 1930s for tournament casting by Marvin Hedge of Portland, Oregon. They became popular among steelheaders, and 1950 saw the first commercial head made available by the Sunset Line and Twine Company of Petaluma, California.

Shooting heads certainly are adaptable, allowing you to use anything from floating head to pure lead-core dredgers to fish anywhere in the water column. I find heads to be a great asset for much of my inshore needs. The two most widely used for inshore saltwater fishing are Type 4 and Type 6 heads. I would also highly recommend carrying a lead-core LC-13 head. Commercially made shooting heads tend to come in 30-foot and 38-foot lengths. Anglers also routinely make their own custom heads by splicing together various full-line tapers or by shortening commercial heads. I've seen custom heads varying in length from 10 feet to 40 feet. These custom designs are built to suit personal casting and angling styles. I prefer to use lengths in the range of 26 to 32 feet.

Running lines to use behind these shooting heads can be either coated or uncoated. Consider the sink rate, stretch, and handling qualities of the material. Uncoated lines include various monofilament or PVC (polyvinyl chloride) designs. The mono called Amnesia is a classic choice of anglers who use monofilament running lines. Most fly fishers use Amnesia in 20-pound, 25-pound, and 30-pound test sizes. It's worth the effort to find clear mono running line, which tangles less, though it will seem limper because the dyes used to color mono add stiffness. Monofilament will offer you a line that cuts through the water with minimal resistance. It would be smart to change this material at least once a season. Fresh monofilament is cheap insurance against the effects of ultraviolet radiation and the accumulation of nicks and cuts. Other uncoated running lines that offer less stretch and that wear well include the newer PVC models that come in oval and flat-beam configurations. They're hard, slick, and have an extremely low coefficient of friction. They come in 35-pound and 50-pound test sizes. I've found the 35-pound line to be ideal for West Coast fisheries. Just be aware that all uncoated running lines coil to some degree, and they all tangle at some point. Get used to it. It's really no big deal most of the time. Make a habit of stretching monofilament or PVC running lines before you start your day on the water. Continue to monitor the material and stretch any segments that appear to be curling after use.

Coated lines can be braided materials or simply variations of the materials used in regular fly lines. They probably have the best feel during a retrieve. They're also easy to track visually. They're currently available in diameters of .027 inches through .035 inches.

Many flats anglers prefer sink-tip lines for fishing under conditions that require stealthy presentations. These are full-line designs sporting very short sinking tips, not the longer integrated shooting head and running line styles. Typically, the sinking section is no longer than 10 feet. These lines can also be quite productive working in the intertidal zone and jetty habitats.

LEADER AND TIPPETS

Leader systems can be pretty straightforward for inshore work. Some days, all you need is a simple, straight piece of leader tied directly to the fly. Other times, you might want to incorporate a lighter tippet section for stealth or elasticity. Occasionally, you may wish to add an abrasion resistant shock trace or bite tippet. Don't bog yourself down with elaborate formulas when fishing for the species covered in this book, though. Commercial hand-tied or knotless tapered leaders are just fine.

Salty gamefish and the abusive habitats they frequent require a slightly different approach to selecting leader material. Instead of using breaking strength as your primary criterion, select your leaders by determining a material's diameter and resistance to abrasion. Generally speaking, it requires a larger-diameter leader to handle heavy or bulky flies. It's easier to cast in windy conditions with large-diameter leaders and tippets, too. Fishing for toothy critters or pulling your fly through sharp mussel beds and around abrasive pilings demands larger-diameter leaders for protection. That's why you'll find the fly-fishing industry offers saltwater leader materials with diameters larger than their freshwater counterparts.

Leader and tippet materials currently are composed of either tough nylon monofilament (often complex copolymers) or fluorocarbon (polyvinylidenflouride, or PVDF). Fluorocarbon has a refractory index closer to that of water, making it less visible to gamefish. It is unaffected by ultraviolet light, unlike mono, and sinks faster than mono. However, fluorocarbon is rather brittle and requires specific knots. A four-turn Surgeon's Knot is one of the best. The standard Clinch Knot, Uni-Knot, and Palomar are three more choices that work well with this material.

Breaking strengths still count as a consideration in your choice of leaders and tippets, but not for the obvious reason—not for the amount of strain you can expect a leader to take. I use the leader's breaking strength to help me establish elasticity in my tackle system. I also choose a breaking strength that allows me to break my fly off if necessary.

If you prefer to build your own leaders, here are a few pointers. Butt sections of 20-pound, 30-pound, and 35-pound material are ideal. I usually reserve the lighter material for my 6-weight outfits. No matter what the rod weight, I like to keep the butt lengths around 3 to 4 feet on my saltwater leaders. Using a loop-to-loop system, I often attach a straight tippet section of 4 to 5 feet. If I need a leader that is more precisely tapered, I usually turn to the commercial knotless leaders.

When it comes to tippet materials, what I use depends on what species I'm targeting. I use 8-pound or 10-pound-test material for silversides, surfperch, and pink and sockeye salmon, 10-pound or 12 -pound test for Pacific mackerel, sand bass, rockfish, and estuary flatfish, 12-pound or 16-pound test for coho and chum salmon, skipjacks, bonito, barracudas, and surf-zone flatfish, and 16-pound or 20-pound test for king salmon, striped bass, white seabass, kelp bass, leopard and smoothhound sharks, and blue sharks

If you need shock traces or bite tippets, the most popular materials include the same materials I use for constructing butt sections—20-pound through 35-pound-test mono.

MISCELLANEOUS GEAR

Stripping baskets and buckets—sometimes I love 'em, sometimes I hate 'em. They can help make fishing possible under some conditions, or complicate matters to a point of high frustration. Mostly, I think, they complicate matters, but there are enough variables in fly fishing to consider the good points of stripping baskets and buckets, too. In some specific conditions, stripping baskets and buckets could contribute to your success. You just need to know when it's advantageous to use them, and when it's best to leave them at home.

My two biggest concerns involve the use of baskets. These tools are typically worn around the waist by wading anglers. The Pacific is a very dynamic environment—some might even call it violent. The changes in conditions are so dramatic that an angler without a care in the world one moment can be in extreme danger the next. An improperly used basket can quickly become an anchor in the surf zone if an unforeseen wave strikes, knocking a wading fly fisher off balance and filling the basket with water, hindering efforts at recovery.

My second concern focuses on angling techniques. The basket's posi-

Be sure to practice with your basket before you hit the beach.
PHOTOGRAPH BY GLENN KISHI

tion can limit your choice of retrieve styles. If it gets in the way of long pulls, for example, it restricts the ways you can impart life to your fly. It also can become the focus of your attention, instead of the fishing itself or the surf environment, as you try to strip line into it. The techniques that matter most involve catching fish, not placing line in neat coils in a stripping basket. It takes an astute fly fisher to become adept at managing this equipment in the conditions that prevail on any given day in the field.

Sometimes, though, stripping baskets and buckets can facilitate line management and rod and reel storage. Under the proper conditions, the use of buckets or baskets can protect your outfits and increase your efficiency in field techniques.

Baskets originally were designed for river wading. Northwest steelheaders, who frequently need to make long casts, used baskets to store their loose, coiled line and reduce river drag when casting. Saltwater anglers soon discovered the benefits of this simple device for working in the surf zone and in jetty environments. Saltwater flyrodders embraced the use of this equipment wholeheartedly, even though it's now pretty rare to see a basket in use on a river.

When you decide to fish with a stripping basket, in most situations, it's often best to wear the basket slightly off your hip, rather than centered under your belly. You don't want the basket to act like a water trap or take the full force of a wave. I've seen plenty of anglers doubled over in the surf zone by a basket that became filled with water. Hip placement positions the basket out of the surge and lessens the impact of breaking surf or heavy currents. Which side you wear it on, though, shouldn't just be dictated by whether you're right-handed or left-handed. Wading anglers, particularly on estuary flats, need to adjust the basket depending on the direction of the current. Wading against the current will favor a side-hip position that keeps the basket away from the direct impact of the flow. For down-current wading, you can position the basket centrally under your belly. Retrieves that involve longer strips, requiring a pendulum, full-arm movement are better served with the basket in a hip position. Shorter strips using just the wrist work with the basket in most any position.

Whatever you do, don't let putting your line in the stripping basket become so engrossing that you forget you're fishing. Don't miss strikes because you were more concerned with hitting the basket than setting the hook! As I mentioned before, these tools can help you or hinder you. If you need to use a stripping basket for the fishing you do, find a good practice area and become familiar with the mechanics of this equipment. Familiarity with the basket and with the stripping techniques it requires will bolster your productivity.

Basket designs can vary. You'll find both solid plastic and pliable mesh styles available commercially. Before you plunk down any cash, though, ask yourself if the basket is suitable for the environments you frequent. Mesh designs shed water more quickly, are lightweight, and have frames that can be molded for a custom fit. Some are collapsible for ease of packing. Solid plastic models can take a real beating, and the plastic isn't susceptible to mildew or rot. Plastic designs featuring "fingers" or "cones" in the bed help minimize line tangles. Virtually all commercially produced baskets have belts with quick-release buckles and large, comfortable webbing.

Most do-it-yourselfers use a variation on the solid plastic theme. Simple conversions of products such as Tupperware containers or wash basins can produce a very effective basket. Just be sure your own conversion creates a basket that sheds water rapidly. As for belts, I've seen everything used from bungee cords to climbing rope. Personally, I feel you can't beat the qualities of a good wading belt made from Cordura nylon or neoprene with a quick-release Delrin buckle for safety in case you need to ditch the basket quickly.

In a boat, fly fishing from a sitting position is by no means comfortable with something bulky around your waist. Buckets, instead of stripping baskets, however, can be a real benefit. And if you fish while standing in a boat, buckets can again complement your needs. Five-gallon paint containers, wire mesh wastepaper bins, even small plastic garbage cans will perform beautifully for you. There now are commercially available stripping buckets with non-skid bases made especially for fly fishers, as well.

Using a stripping bucket in a boat will give you maximum freedom in choosing stripping techniques, allowing you to be much more aggressive if an exaggerated retrieve is required to entice the fish. Another nice perk that comes from using a bucket in a boat is that doubles as a rod holder. The bucket can be your staging area. Line can be premeasured and draped into the container as you travel between fishing spots, the rod positioned for a quick grab, and everything made ready to deliver the fly in the most expeditious manner.

There are two more items of gear that could make your saltwater fly-fishing outings a true success. To help you better control the gamefish,

Ed Berg uses a simple laundry basket to help manage his line.
PHOTOGRAPH BY KEN HANLEY

and facilitate proper handling technique, you'll need an aid that restrains your catch and one that promotes a quick hook retrieval.

The Boga Grip is a tool for controlling a feisty saltwater gamefish as you land them. Its unique, spring-loaded clamp uses the fish's body weight and movement to secure a hold against the lower jaw. If the fish

The author uses a Boga Grip to help revive and release a rockfish.
PHOTOGRAPH BY GLENN KISHI

continues to roll or thrash about, the clamp will freely rotate, applying consistent pressure on the fish, rather torque against your wrist and arm. If you wish to weigh your catch, the Boga has a built-in scale.

When you're removing the hook, keeping your hands well away from toxic spines and sharp teeth is a smart idea, too. Be sure to carry a device that helps you extract hooks. Hemostats and pliers are standard choices. Just make sure they're long enough and heavy enough to get the job done. Another option is the Ketchum Release Tool, Saltwater Series. It's simply a long handle with a slotted, cylindrical head. The head slides down your leader line to engage and trap the hook. It's a trusty old idea that's been upgraded for the better.

WHEN IT COMES TO PRESENTING your fly and retrieving it, the best advice I can give you is to stay flexible and be willing to adapt your tackle and tactics to the conditions you find. Along with the tips presented in each of the species chapters, the following recommendations should give you a good general overview of techniques for achieving success afield. There are several basic techniques that anyone can use, whether they're fishing on foot or from a boat.

The "tip-down" position gives increased sensitivity and line control.
PHOTOGRAPH BY GLENN KISHI

THE TIP-DOWN RETRIEVE

This is an essential technique for what I call puppeteering a fly—manipulating it in a lifelike manner. I find myself using it 95 percent of the time I'm fishing in salt water, and it's important for freshwater angling, as well. Since most saltwater fishing involves swimming streamers or crawling flies through various kinds of cover on sinking lines, keeping the rod tip low significantly increases your control during the retrieve. The tip-down position is highly effective for poppers and floating lines, as well, though. A tip-down retrieve keeps the fly line down out of the wind, helping you stay in touch with the fly throughout the entire retrieve path and increasing sensitivity by eliminating most of the slack in your line. By actually placing the rod tip under the surface, as I often do, the water also helps cushion against extreme shocks when fish strike and positions your rod for a stronger strip strike.

THE SINGLE-HAND PENDULUM RETRIEVE

Erratic movement that mimics the behavior of injured prey can trigger strikes when you're fishing with baitfish imitations. Single-hand retrieves are extremely productive ways to impart a convincing, lifelike motion to a fly. The technique is extremely flexible, allowing you to mix subtle, short strips that result in movements of a few inches with arm's-length pendulum pulls that produce explosive spurts close to four feet in length. No other stripping technique provides you the capability to move the fly in so many ways. You can even increase the distance the fly travels by sweeping your rod tip away from your stripping hand while you complete a full pendulum pull. And pausing between single-hand strips creates a jigging motion that persuasively mimics injured and disoriented prey. No matter where you position the rod, close to your body or reaching out to clear waves and obstructions, you'll always be able to employ the widest array of strip lengths. It's pretty tough to beat the adaptability of the single-hand retrieve technique.

THE DOUBLE OVERHAND RETRIEVE

This tactic requires you to place the rod butt under your arm. The reel should be positioned in a way that doesn't hinder its spool from revolving. Pinning the rod against your torso allows both hands to control the fly line and maintain maximum contact with your fly. Since you continually alternate stripping hands, there's never a moment in the retrieve when you're not in contact with the fly line and the fly.

Contrary to what most people think, the double overhand retrieve really excels with ultraslow presentations. Creeping crustaceans through a maze of grass or slithering a worm over kelp holdfasts and around mussel beds demands a high degree of touch. Without consistent contact, it's hard to know when changes occur in the topography or type of cover you're working. In addition, the strike could be subtle from a fish tracking a slow-moving fly. It's great for situations that don't favor visual clues, but rather depend on tactile information.

The double overhand retrieve frequently is assumed to be the way to

The double-overhand: perfect for ultraslow or sustained, speedy retrieves.
PHOTOGRAPH BY KEN HANLEY

make a fly move really fast, and indeed, the technique facilitates a sustained, rapid retrieve. But these quick retrieves minimize jigging action, and that up-and-down really attracts fish. Also, because of your rod's position, you can't give the fly the extreme burst of speed you can with a single-hand pendulum pull. You will, however, have the ability to achieve a rapid cadence that creates the impression of a sustained flight.

THE TIP-DOWN/BUTT-HIGH FIGHTING POSITION

If you've never caught one of the saltwater gamefish, you're in for a real treat. Their strength-to-weight ratio is amazing. Saltwater predators, even the most diminutive species, are no match for the unprepared. Accordingly, saltwater flyrodders need to master a rod-handling technique that really helps control a catch. A low rod tip increases pressure on the fish. So does elevating the rod butt to an equal or higher plane than the tip. This inverted, tip-down/butt high position results in a more direct force applied to the hook by reducing the angle between the rod and the line. Conversely, the higher you place the rod tip, the less pressure you apply on the hook. If you work with ultralight tippets, this high-tip position is necessary to maximize the tippet's chances for transferring shock and stress. But the tip-down/butt-high position drives the load farther down the rod and protects the tip from stress failure. Instead of using the rod solely to absorb shock, you now can use the rod as a lever to fight the fish, never letting the quarry rest or recuperate.

Anticipating last-minute antics, I try to keep the tip down and the

The author gains maximum leverage with a "tip-down/butt-high" technique.
PHOTOGRAPH BY GLENN KISHI

butt up until the final moments of landing my catch. If the fish jumps, I also "bow to the fish" by dropping the tip straight toward it. If my quarry decides to take a deepwater dive, I simply let my rod tip follow under the surface to absorb the sudden shock.

You won't need to exert maximum pressure on every fish you catch. However, training yourself to use the tip-down / butt-high fighting position in conjunction with the tip-down retrieve lets you start to retrieve every cast and fight every fish from a position of control.

FISH THE DOWN-CURRENT SIDE OF STRUCTURE AND COVER

Learn to let the tide and current be part of your delivery system. The natural flow around or over obstacles creates a perfect environment for

Fish the down-current side of structure or cover. It shifts with the tide.
PHOTOGRAPH BY GLENN KISHI

The tide cycle helps to establish which side to fish.
PHOTOGRAPH BY KEN HANLEY

predators to intercept prey. Think like a stream angler for a moment. In a stream, the prime ambush stations often are located on the down-current side of ledges, logs, and rocks. You can use the same principle to locate fish in much of the inshore environment—with one major difference. The tide will dictate changes in the current's direction of flow. The "down-current" side reverses with every shift in the tide. To be effective, you need to pay attention to signs of those shifting currents. You can't simply approach an area from the same side all day long. Both the bait and gamefish reorient themselves as the tide floods or ebbs.

WORK THE EDGES OF SHALLOW OR DEEP HABITAT

You can always count on these edges and boundary zones to concentrate prey and the predators that follow them. The tide once again helps to determine the direction from which you'll work. I prefer to cast my fly first into the shallow habitat whenever possible. I won't need to sink the offering for any lengthy period. Gamefish usually enter the shallows on the prowl. If I don't elicit any immediate strikes, I continue to retrieve my fly over the edge, into deeper water. Once the fly crosses that boundary zone from shallow to deep, I let it stall for a brief moment, then drop down to a new level. It's a high-percentage move that also keeps me in control of the fly. The more dramatic the change in depth, the less likely I'll have to move the fly any great distance away from that boundary zone. Predators hiding below have light, current, temperature, and tide in their favor.

FISH SLOWER DEEPER, FASTER ON TOP

The closer you work your presentation to the bottom, the slower your fly should move and the shorter the movements should be. If you were a member of a bottom-dwelling prey species, rapid movement would tend to draw the attention of fish that would regard you as dinner. It's not a sound strategy, unless it's necessary to negotiate short areas of open space between rocks, grass beds, pilings, or whatever else usually provides cover. So most of the creatures that predators seek tend to creep, crawl, slither, or swim slowly and hesitatingly. So should your fly. Of course, a few quick scurries could always spice things up.

Surface-oriented species often live in a frenetic world. Prey populations living higher in the water column are more dependent upon rapid and erratic flight to stay alive. In many cases, only evasion can save them from predation. Baitfish and squid also use schooling as a defense. Gamefish are tuned into this behavior and seek disoriented and injured prey. Long and short bursts of speed, interspersed with short pauses, draw attention to your fly. Keep your offering on the move, and make the predator commit to stopping its escape.

There's at least one exception to the rapid-fire surface approach: when you're working with krill and various euphausiid imitations. These tiny creatures are basically drifters. Consider them your dry flies of the salt. Make the cast, mend your line, if necessary, then simply let the fly float in a dead drift. Imparting an occasional subtle twitch is a nice complementary move. Salmon and other gamefish can key on the easy pickings this particular food resource provides.

THE UP-CURRENT, SINKING-LINE PRESENTATION

Using the current and tide to assist you with depth control is a smart, efficient way to get your fly into your target zone. If you turn and face directly into the current, then cast your fly into the approaching flow, you're making what's commonly referred to as an "up-current" presentation. The force of the water drives your sinking line under the surface immediately. It continues to produce slack as it drifts back toward you, which allows the fly and line to sink. As your line gets closer and ultimately drops straight below your casting station, you'll achieve maximum depth. If you allow the line to continue past this position, it now begins to swing upward. This technique works best in a boat. Anglers on foot can execute the tactic, but the results tend to be less dramatic.

THE NINETY-DEGREE SWING, FLOATING/SINKING PRESENTATION

If an up-current, deep presentation isn't what you're looking for, casting across the current allows you to work from the surface down to moderate depths. This is an outstanding choice when you're using floating or intermediate lines to swim streamers or sinking lines to reach middle depths. By casting ninety degrees to the current flow, you get some drag with a surface-buoyed fly line. The result is a tight-line presentation that limits the drop zone of the fly. Anglers who want to increase the working distance of flies cast across the current can simply incorporate a few roll-cast mends late in the swing. To produce a slightly deeper swing, add slack immediately after making the cast.

THE DOWN-CURRENT, FLOATING/SINKING PRESENTATION

Casting down-current works best for presentations that are surface-oriented. It creates immediate resistance on the fly line. This technique is perfect for floating and intermediate lines with poppers or surface-running streamers. Depending on the current's strength, sinking lines will position themselves anywhere from subsurface to within a few feet of the surface. I can remember fishing strong rip lines that required a lead-core head. The bass were feeding on baitfish concentrated in the heavy flow. The sinking head kept my streamer approximately two feet under the surface throughout the entire retrieve. It was the magic zone where all the action took place that day. The fish rarely fed deeper and weren't willing to bust the surface. Casting a heavy sinking line, but using a down-current presentation gave me optimal control for establishing the proper depth and retrieve path.

Anchovies and sardines are key prey species throughout the Pacific.

PHOTOGRAPH BY GLENN KISHI

WHETHER YOU'RE WADING IN THE SURF LINE or working open waters from a skiff, you need to know the principal food items in the diets of the Pacific's saltwater predators.

Here are sixteen of the most common marine munchies you'll want your flies to imitate when fishing the estuaries, bays, and beaches of the Pacific, along with fly patterns that imitate them. Patterns were selected based on their size, silhouette, color, and motion.

OPALESCENT SQUID (*LOLIGO OPALESCENS*)

Just about any predator species that swims in the Pacific ocean dines on squid. You'll find these sleek swimmers in both open water and inshore, relatively close to kelp beds when they breed, from December through April.

The squid's body is full and round, tapering down from front to back. Its principal colors are white, gold, and gray. Squid are usually mottled or speckled with brownish black spots.

Fly patterns should range from approximately four to seven inches in length. Eyes on these patterns are important, since the creatures have large, prominently placed eyes.

Sample fly patterns: Rabbit-Strip Fly (all-white), size 2/0 to 4/0; Sea Arrow Squid, size 2/0 to 4/0; and the Tres Generation Popper, size 1/0 to 4/0.

Principal predators: tuna, striped bass, white seabass, blue sharks, rockfish, and calico bass.

THE NORTHERN ANCHOVY (*ENGRAULIS MORDAX*)

The northern anchovy is probably the most common schooling baitfish along the Pacific coastline. It can be found just about anywhere between Queen Charlotte Island and southern Baja in both inshore and nearshore environments. It is even pelagic at times. Both immature "pinheads" and adults provide hardy fare for West Coast gamefish.

Flies should range from two to seven inches in length. The fish is usually blue or green across the back and sports a silvery white body.

Sample fly patterns: ALF Baitfish, size 1/0 to 3/0; Clouser Minnow, size 2 to 1/0; Pearl Yeti, size 2; Deep Candy Bendback, size 1/0; Lefty's

Deceiver (green/white, olive/white, or blue/white), size 1/0 to 3/0; Sea Habit Bucktail, size 1/0 to 3/0.

Principal predators: salmon, white seabass, rockfish, tuna, bonito, blue sharks, calico bass, barracudas, striped bass, sand bass, and halibut.

The Slough Anchovy (*Anchoa delicatissima*)

Found predominately in Southern California and Baja, this species prefers protected habitat. You'll likely find it cruising around estuaries and inner bays.

The slough anchovy is a small baitfish. The adults are typically less than four inches in length. Fly patterns of two to three inches are ideal. Slough anchovies have a green back, a prominent silver side stripe, and white lower half.

Sample fly patterns: Deep Candy Bendback, size 1/0; Clouser Minnow, size 2; Fatal Attraction, size 2 to 4; Lefty's Deceiver, size 2; and Pearl Yeti, size 2 to 5.

Principal predators: barracudas, sand bass, white seabass, calico bass, and halibut.

The Deepbody Anchovy (*Anchoa compressa*)

As the name suggests, this baitfish is broader from dorsal fin to belly than the northern or slough anchovies. The "DB" anchovy frequents the coast from central California south into Baja. It can be found in protected environments such as estuaries and harbors, as well as in more open shoreline haunts.

The deepbody anchovy is tall, narrow from side to side, and not very long. Patterns three to five inches in length are a good choice. The fish often has an olive back and a broad silver stripe on its side.

Sample fly patterns: ALF Baitfish, size 2 to 1/0; Flashtail Whistler (red/white and SPS), size 1/0.

Principal predators: sand bass, white seabass, striped bass, and halibut.

The Pacific Sardine (*Sardinops sagax*)

These are rather large baitfish, generally around twelve inches or longer. Though they roam the open ocean, sardines are frequently encountered by inshore predators such as sharks and small tuna. The baitfish have a dark back that's typically blue or green. Their sides and bellies tend to be silver. You'll find the Pacific sardine sporting a random pattern of dark spots on its upper side. Fly patterns used to imitate this species should be as long as possible. Seven to nine inches would be ideal under most conditions.

Sample fly patterns: Lefty's Deceiver, size 3/0 to 4/0; Sea Habit Bucktail, size 3/0 to 4/0.

Principal predators: Sharks, striped bass, barracudas, white seabass.

THE PACIFIC SAND LANCE (*AMMODYTES HEXAPTERUS*)

Anglers from Alaska to Oregon can tap into the bounty of this baitfish species. The sand lance travels in large schools throughout the inshore realm. It's a frequent visitor to the intertidal zone.

The fish has a distinct metallic look overall. Its back can be blue or green. Its sides and lower body are definitely silver. Though it can grow to approximately eight inches long, fly patterns of four inches or less are most productive. Imitations should be elongated and lean.

Sample fly patterns: Clouser Minnow, size 1/0; Deep Candy Bendback, size 1/0; Jensen Foam Slider, size 2; Lefty's Deceiver, size 1/0; and Sorcerer's Touch, size 2.

Principal predators: salmon, rockfish, and halibut.

THE PACIFIC HERRING (*CLUPEA PALLASII*)

Herring are one of the staples on the menu of open-water predators. You'll encounter them from Alaska to Baja, but they're rare south of central California. Green or olive covers their backs, with silver and grayish tones underneath. These are large baitfish, but don't let that observation mislead you. It's the young that are most vulnerable to inshore predation.

During their winter-spring spawning cycle, you can find the adult females in protected shallow waters. Pay particular attention to grass beds and kelp habitat, because this is where the eggs are deposited. The newborn will use this cover as a nursery. In the spring and summer, inshore predators begin to key on the young herring. Small, silvery fly patterns about two to three inches in length can be very effective.

Sample fly patterns: Pearl Yeti, size 2 to 4; Deep Candy Bendback, size 1/0; Clouser Minnow, size 2; and ALF Baitfish, size 2.

Principal predators: salmon, rockfish, halibut, and striped bass.

SHINER PERCH (*CYMATOGASTER AGGREGATA*)

These little gems are a cornerstone bait in any shallow-water environment. They're especially abundant around eelgrass beds and various built cover such as pilings and docks. Their range extends from southeast

Alaska down into northern Baja. A shiner perch's body is somewhat narrow from side to side and elliptical, like a serving platter, from head to tail. Overall, they're silver and gray. A series of small, dark spots can be found on their flanks.

Small to medium-sized fly patterns three to five inches long work best. Imitations should be tall from dorsal to belly, narrow from side to side, and short from nose to tail.

Sample fly patterns: Flashtail Whistler (SPS), size 1/0 to 3/0; ALF Baitfish, size 3/0; and Sea Habit Bucktail, size 2/0 to 3/0.

Principal predators: striped bass, salmon, halibut, and white seabass.

SCULPINS (*COTTIDAE*)

These bottom dwellers are found in the diet of most shore predators that prefer rocky and tidepool habitats. Sculpins are large-headed, squat-bodied, mottled fish from two to eight inches in length. Any combination of darker colors would be appropriate in your fly pattern. Purple, brown, yellow, black, and olive seem to dominate in most species.

Sample fly patterns and principal predator species are the same for both sculpins and plainfin midshipmen. Sample fly patterns: Lefty's Deceiver (red/yellow or all-yellow), size 2 to 2/0; Rabbit-Strip Fly (brown), size 2 to 1/0; and the Near 'Nuff Sculpin, size 4.

Principal predators: striped bass, leopard sharks, halibut, and rockfish.

THE PLAINFIN MIDSHIPMAN (*PORICHTHYS NOTATUS*)

Midshipmen are a common baitfish found in bays and estuaries from southeast Alaska to the Gulf of California. This species prefers rocky and muddy habitat. This is a great baitfish to imitate when they begin their spawning cycle in the shallows. Usually spawning activity peaks in the early summer.

The fish has a purple or dark brown back. Its flanks and belly are usually yellowish. Its body is elongated, with a steady taper as you near the tail fin. Flies should range from three to seven inches in length.

Sample fly patterns and principal predators: see the listing for sculpins above.

THE PACIFIC MOLE CRAB (*EMERITA ANALOGA*)

A plump and prolific crustacean, this should be the number-one choice for fly fishers working the surf zone. Unlike other crabs, which are flattened in cross section and oval, the sand crab is rounded and egglike.

Color commonly varies from olive to gray on most mole crabs, but when they are in their soft-shell molting stage, they're cream or light tan.

Smaller fly patterns around an inch to an inch and a half long best imitate this little guy. Adding a bit of red or orange to the underside simulates the roe sac and makes the pattern especially attractive to hungry predators.

Sample fly patterns: the Surf Grub, size 6 to 10; Labyrinth Crab (bleached, tan, or olive), size 2; and Near 'Nuff Sculpin, size 4.

Principal predators: surfperch, striped bass, sand bass, and halibut.

THE PURPLE SHORE CRAB (*HEMIGRAPSUS NUDUS*)

This small crab has the classic look you expect of a crab. It's generally found among rocks, kelp, sea grasses, and gravel. It inhabits most shoreline environments. The crab's body is flat, and about twice as wide as it is long. Imitations should be approximately one to two inches in length. The shore crab's colors are predominantly dark above. Purple and black cover the shell's back. Variations could include reddish brown or greenish yellow. The underside is often light cream or white.

Sample fly patterns: Labyrinth Crab (purple, brown, or red), size 1/0.

Principal predators: surfperch, striped bass, sand bass, and halibut.

THE CLAM WORM (*NEREIS VIRENS*)

You might call it gross, but bait fishers call it magic. No matter what we think about its looks, this worm is dinner for a number of inshore gamefish. The clam worm prefers sand, mud, and sea grasses. It's a super choice to imitate when you're fishing protected waters.

The worm's coloring can be a combination of green and brown on the back with highlights of gold and red underneath. Your imitation should be long, lean, and flattened. The most effective patterns are approximately five to seven inches overall.

Sample fly pattern: the V-Worm, size 6.

Principal predators: halibut, flounder, striped bass, and sand bass.

SIX-LINED NEMERTEAN (*TUBULANUS SEXLINEATUS*)

This little worm is a streamlined inhabitant of mussel beds, rocks, and pilings. It has a thin body covered mostly in black or brown. As the name suggests, at least six white longitudinal stripes are present. Your fly patterns should be kept lean and under six inches in length.

Sample fly pattern: the V-Worm, size 10.

Principal predators: striped bass and sand bass.

GHOST SHRIMP (*CALLIANASSA AFFINIS* AND *CALLIANASSA CALIFORNIENSIS*)

Ghost shrimp live on the beach from Southern California down to Baja. They also live in the bays and estuaries all the way from southeast Alaska to Baja. You can expect to find them burrowed in sand and burrowed in mud. These chunky shrimp come in colors ranging from white to pink, with touches of yellow. Their bodies are round and fairly long. Imitations should be from two to five inches in length.

Sample fly pattern: Jay's Grass Shrimp, size 2 to 4.

Principal predators: surfperch, halibut, flounders, and sand bass.

GRASS SHRIMP

Let's consider this a grouping, rather than any individual species to imitate. A wide collection of shrimp species live among the eelgrass beds, tide pools, and rocky crevices of the Pacific shoreline. These shrimp share a common coloration, tending toward pale green. Many have a transparent quality. "Grass shrimp" are delicate creatures, usually small, with a classic shrimp profile. Fly patterns should be no longer than one and a half inches in length.

Sample fly patterns: Jay's Grass Shrimp, size 4; CDC Shrimp (white or olive), size 4; Clouser Minnow (olive/white), size 4; and Diamond Shrimp (white), size 5.

Principal predators: mackerel, silversides, surfperch, rockfish, sand bass, and flounders.

That's quite a collection of tasty treats to tempt and tease saltwater fish in West Coast estuaries and bays and along the Pacific's beaches. They swim backward or forward, walk sideways, tumble along, and even slither. They're wild, sometimes weird, and always highly effective for attracting a predator to your line.

The Sorcerer's Touch.
PHOTOGRAPH BY GLENN KISHI

PACIFIC MACKEREL

Clouser Minnow (blue/white, olive/white, or gray/white), size 2, 1/0.

ALF Baitfish, size 2, 2/0.

Pearl Yeti, size 2, 5.

Deep Candy Bendback (olive), size 2, 1/0.

SILVERSIDES (TOPSMELT AND JACKSMELT)

CDC Shrimp (golden olive, tan, or white), size 4, 6, 8, 10.

Diamond Shrimp (pearl or gold), size 4, 6.

SURFPERCH

Surfpercher Red, size 2, 4.

Surf Grub, size 10, 6.

Rusty Squirrel Clouser, size 4, 6.

Micro Shrimp, size 6.

Jay's Grass Shrimp, size 4.

Near 'Nuff Sculpin, size 4, 6.

ROCKFISH

Lefty's Deceiver (blue/white, green/white, or olive/white), size 1/0, 3/0.
ALF Baitfish, size 2, 2/0.
Sea Habit Bucktail, size 2/0, 3/0.
Tropical Punch, size 2/0.
Rabbit-Strip Fly (white, brown, purple, or black), size 1/0.
Sea Arrow Squid, size 2/0, 4/0.
Gold Buccaneer, size 2, 1/0.
Labyrinth Crab, size 1/0.
Clouser Minnow (olive/white or gray/white), size 2, 1/0.
Jay's Grass Shrimp, size 4.

PACIFIC SALMON

Sea Habit Bucktail, size 1/0, 3/0.
ALF Baitfish, size 2, 1/0, 2/0.
Fatal Attraction (green/chartreuse), size 2, 4.
Green Comet, size 2, 8.
Sorcerer's Touch, size 2, 4.
Salmon Waker, size 2.
Pink Pollywog, size 2.
Pearl Yeti, size 2, 5.
Diamond Shrimp (pearl, pink, or gold), size 5, 7.
CDC Shrimp (pink, tan, white, brown, or golden olive), size 4, 8.
Jensen Foam Slider, size 2.
Horner Deer-Hair Shrimp, size 4.
Sockeye Boss, size 4, 8.
Sea Arrow Squid, size 2/0, 4/0.
Sockeye Special, size 6, 8.

CALIFORNIA HALIBUT

Gold Buccaneer, size 2, 1/0.
Lefty's Deceiver (blue/white, white, or red/yellow), size 1/0, 3/0.
Deep Candy Bendback (olive), size 1/0.
Clouser Minnow (chartreuse/white or brown/white), size 2, 1/0.

STARRY FLOUNDER

Jay's Grass Shrimp, size 4.
Labyrinth Crab, size 2.
Clouser Minnow (brown/white or olive/white), size 2, 4.
Deep Candy Bendback (olive), size 2, 4.

STRIPED BASS

Clouser Minnow (olive/white), size 1/0.

Sea Habit Bucktail, size 2/0, 3/0.

Flashtail Whistler (SPS [Shiner Perch Simulation], red/white, or black), size 1/0, 3/0.

ALF Baitfish, size 2/0, 3/0.

Jay's Grass Shrimp, size 4.

Labyrinth Crab, size 2.

V-Worm, size 6.

Various poppers or sliders, size 2, 2/0.

BLUE SHARK

Sea Arrow Squid, size 4/0.

Lefty's Deceiver (white, blue/white, or red/white), size 2/0, 4/0.

Flashtail Whistler (SPS or red/white), size 3/0, 4/0.

LEOPARD SHARK AND SMOOTHHOUND SHARK

Sea Arrow Squid, size 2/0.

Clouser Minnow (brown/white or brown/yellow), size 2, 1/0.

Deep Candy Bendback (olive or brown), size 1/0.

Jay's Grass Shrimp, size 4.

Labyrinth Crab, size 2.

SAND BASS AND KELP BASS

Rabbit-Strip Fly (white, brown, or purple), size 2, 1/0.

Clouser Minnow (brown/white or olive/white), size 2, 1/0, 4/0.

ALF Baitfish, size 2, 1/0.

Sea Arrow Squid, size 2/0, 3/0.

Deep Candy Bendback (olive or brown), size 1/0.

WHITE SEABASS

Lefty's Deceiver (white or blue/white), size 1/0, 3/0.

Clouser Minnow (gray/white), size 1/0, 3/0.

Flashtail Whistler (SPS or red/white), size 1/0, 3/0.

Sea Habit Bucktail, size 1/0, 3/0.

Sea Arrow Squid, size 2/0, 4/0.

CALIFORNIA BARRACUDA

Deep Candy Bendback (olive), size 1/0.

Clouser Minnow (blue/white, olive/white, or green/white), size 2, 1/0.

ALF Baitfish, size 2, 3/0.

BLACK SKIPJACK TUNA

Tres Generation Popper (squid or pearl), size 1/0, 4/0.

Sea Habit Bucktail, size 2/0, 3/0.

ALF Baitfish, size 1/0, 3/0.

Sea Arrow Squid, size 2/0, 4/0.

PACIFIC BONITO

Pearl Yeti, size 2.

Clouser Minnow (chartreuse/white, gray/white, or olive/white),
    size 2, 1/0.

Deep Candy Bendback (olive), size 2, 1/0.

ALF Baitfish, size 2, 1/0.

PART 4
WATERCRAFT

A PATCHWORK OF SEALSKINS stretched around a wooden skeleton, the original Native American kayak provided efficient access to the ocean environment. Today's high-tech kayaks still do. The saltwater fly-fishing community is the most recent to discover the kayak as a way to explore kelp beds, estuaries, the surf zone, and even backcountry tidal sloughs.

So, are sea kayaks the ultimate fly-fishing tool? Well . . . yes and no. It's not such a simple question to answer. First, you need to understand what the design offers, and then you need to stay within the craft's limitations. If you accept the fact that there are limitations, you're more likely to maximize the kayak's strengths.

Today's sea kayak hulls are usually built with either fiberglass or linear polyethylene (rotomolded plastic). There are still a number of companies specializing in wood, or wood and cloth designs, however, and collapsible

Don't own one? Kayaks can be rented along the entire Pacific Coast.
PHOTOGRAPH BY KEN HANLEY

kayaks are also available, manufactured with aerospace-grade aluminum frames and covered with high-tech stretch-fabric hulls such as Hypalon. Inflatable kayaks are on the market, but they're not something you'd want to subject to the rigors of the Pacific. Of the two main designs, the fiberglass kayaks are the lightest, typically running around fifty to fifty-five pounds for solo kayaks. Polyethylene plastic craft usually weigh between fifty-eight and sixty-eight pounds. The overall length for most expedition and tripping models is generally fifteen to seventeen feet. Smaller day-touring models can range from nine to fourteen feet.

The longer hulls offer more storage capacity and greater stability in rough waters. The bow design is knifelike and its tip sweeps upward in an exaggerated fashion, creating a thin edge to help cut through waves and chop. The smaller day tripper's bow is rounded, with a less aggressive taper, and is best used only in calm and protected waters.

Cockpit designs vary from one model to another, but ease of access is

Full-deck designs are the safest for cold-water explorations.

PHOTOGRAPH BY KEN HANLEY

not a design criterion. Instead, paddler position and hull integrity are the paramount concerns. Most companies offer at least one model with the capacity for "larger paddlers."

Hull designs also include a variety of deck hatches for gear access and storage. Expedition-style hulls offer at least two topside positions for access. The hatches are generally made from the same material as the hull. Gaskets, latches, and tie-down straps help seal the deck hatch to protect your stowed gear.

"Sit-on-top" designs have become popular for anglers in warmer climates. These offer paddlers quick entry and exit. Depending on which model you choose, storage chambers and numerous lash points are also available with this rotomolded hull.

Maneuvering such a narrow hull can be a bit frustrating for beginning sea kayakers. The kayak's design is meant to incorporate a bit of tilting from side to side. Learning to lean at the right time will actually help you stabilize the craft against wave action or choppy seas. The initial feeling might be "tippy," but the craft's secondary stability (resistance to capsizing) is what makes it such a seaworthy design.

Many larger expedition and tripping sea kayaks increase their efficiency by using a rudder, rather than the paddler's stroke, to steer. The steering system consists of a pair of foot peddles connected to the rudder by a set of cables. Simply applying pressure to one or the other peddle will adjust the rudder's position from left to right. Rudders are most effective when you find yourself paddling in windy conditions. Keep in mind that not all sea kayaks will feature the rudder option.

When it comes to kayaks tracking in a straight line, the longer the keel, the straighter the hull will track. Expedition-length kayaks track best. Shorter hulls tend to pivot with each paddle stroke. The zigzag motion of day-touring models can make you work harder to get to where the fish are feeding.

Inflatable outrigger chambers or solid outriggers can be used to increase the stability of your craft in most situations. The lightest and most adaptable option is a pair of inflatable sponsons. These are sealed vinyl or nylon pockets that attach to the outside of your kayak via a simple harness system next to the cockpit. With minimal effort, you can deploy them in about a minute. They're perfect for fly fishers, because the elongated forty-inch-by-six-inch balloons won't interfere with your angling.

Solid outriggers are built in the style of outriggers on Polynesian canoes, supporting the kayak on just one side. The system requires that the outrigger's hull be supported by two long braces. The braces are approximately four feet in length. This option is less friendly to the needs of fly fishers. The outrigger and braces can pose a problem if you need to work from both sides of the hull to land your catch. So although both of these flotation systems can offer improved safety, when it comes to fly fishing, I'd put my money on the sponson option.

Anyone venturing into the ocean in a kayak also should consider adding flotation bags for an extra measure of safety. The bags fit snugly into the stern and bow compartments of the hull. Not only do they add buoyancy, but they keep the kayak from getting swamped if you have a mishap. Boat retrieval and self-rescue techniques are much easier to complete with flotation devices in the craft.

You can use either standard flotation bags or storage flotation. Storage designs allow you to stow clothing and gear inside each inflated bag. The bags are typically made from tough, urethane-coated or vinyl-coated nylon.

Tackle .placement is one of the toughest problems you need to address while fishing from a sea kayak. If you stow your gear below deck, you can't really fish from the craft. In most cases, you'll be forced to exit the kayak to gain access to your tackle. Inside storage dimensions also limit what you can carry. Therefore, if you plan on fishing from your kayak, topside is the only way to go. Topside storage has a major drawback, though—it's wet, wet, wet!

Don't—I repeat: don't—place a fly rod under those lash-downs on the fore or aft deck of your kayak. Retrieving the rod will be difficult, at best. Instead, build a simple rod rack or rod tube from a long piece of PVC pipe and two pieces of foam. Secure the pipe to the kayak with the deck straps, and use the foam to create two inner sleeves that support the fly rod at each end of the tube. You can leave your fly rod fully rigged inside this simple carrier. The PVC provides protection, too.

A second solution is to use rod racks of molded plastic and foam.

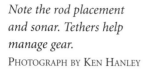

Note the rod placement and sonar. Tethers help manage gear.
PHOTOGRAPH BY KEN HANLEY

This works beautifully if you want to carry several rods. Using a small sheet of Plexiglas approximately eighteen by twenty-four inches as the base, simply secure a pair of rod racks to it. Or you can use the newer rod racks with anodized aluminum rings lined with neoprene sleeves. When you secure the Plexiglas with the deck straps, it will flex and match the hull's contour perfectly. The molded racks will elevate your rods above the tie-downs, allowing free access to the rods. Rod racks won't offer you quite the protection of the PVC pipe carrier, though. Be sure to be careful of your rod tips when you use a rack-style holder. You might want to place the fly rod in the rack with the tip rearward if you use this system.

What about your fly boxes, tippet materials, pliers, and such? Fly fishing vests don't make much sense in a kayak. You need to have unrestricted movement to paddle efficiently, as the makers of the required personal-flotation devices you need to wear when kayaking well know. And a restrictive vest worn over a PFD doesn't make much sense. Small chest packs and deck bags are the solution to this problem.

Chest packs are lightweight and easy to access, but they aren't waterproof. If you're fishing calmer, protected waters, though, this option might suit you just fine. If you find yourself busting through breaking surf or paddling in choppy conditions, however, deck bags are the best solution for tackle storage. The best I've seen on the market are made of urethane-coated nylon and neoprene, with features such as D rings, bungee cords, and stiffened pockets. Deck bags are typically attached to the kayak directly in front of the cockpit. They are meant to take a pounding and keep your gear dry. One alternative to high-tech deck bags, however, is simply to use a heavy-duty map case, a vinyl pouch reinforced with nylon mesh. It provides solid protection for your stored tackle from the rigors of saltwater exposure.

Casting and playing fish while sitting in a kayak require some adaptations in technique. The extremely low casting position is not at all favorable for a long day's fishing with heavy lines and wind-resistant flies. With your legs straight out in front of you and your back in a slightly reclining position, the stress from your casting stroke can add up quickly. Reducing the number of false casts and learning to shoot more line will help. So will using longer rods, positioning your kayak so you can make short to medium casts, and perfecting your roll-casting and water-hauling techniques.

Once you've made the cast, line control can become a source of irritation if you're not thinking ahead. Use the kayak's spray skirt as a stripping apron, letting your line coil on the skirt as if you were using a regular stripping basket. Otherwise, you have to let the line coils fall into the cockpit or onto the ocean's surface. Stripping line into the cockpit won't provide you with an area for efficient line management and makes snags around your legs inevitable. Letting your line rest on the ocean's surface is fine if the water is calm, but you can drift right over the coils and trap them under the hull. Try stripping the line so the coils are trailing you, not in front of you on the drift.

When you're playing and landing your catch, the long, narrow profile of the kayak needs to be parallel to the pull on your line. The closer your rod and line become to being perpendicular to the hull's length, the greater the chances you'll capsize, with the fish helping to pull you over, aided by any sudden movements on your part.

Sea kayaks have been around for ages. Their design is a proven winner for negotiating the seas worldwide. But when it comes to fly fishing, we have a lot to learn in adapting our techniques to these unique craft. Sea kayaking, however, is a growing sport with plenty of expert practitioners. Their experience is especially invaluable when it comes to recommendations about how to stay safe while kayaking Big Blue. The following recommendations for safety gear are from the American Canoe Association National Coastal Kayaking Committee, and California Canoe and Kayak, an outfitter and retail center:

1. Flotation (float bags and/or bulkheads).
2. Personal flotation device (life vest).
3. Bailer or pump.
4. Clothing appropriate for destination.
5. Fresh water (thermos), food.
6. Compass.
7. First-aid kit, sun block, knife (single fixed blade, serrated preferred).
8. Paddle float, paddle leash, self-rescue device.
9. Tide and current tables.
10. Duct tape.
11. Tow rope with a throw bag (a minimum of fifty feet of ¼-inch polypro or Spectra rope).
12. Spare paddle.
13. Signaling device: mirror, whistle, horn, or flare.

I'D JUST CUT THE POWER to my trolling motor and started to position the canoe with a paddle. It barely made a ripple on the estuary's surface. Within seconds, a sea otter appeared just a few feet from the bow. The craft was so quiet that we ran little risk of spooking the creature.

Canoes are terrific for quiet back-bay expeditions.
PHOTOGRAPH BY KEN HANLEY

We continued to glide past a congregation of wading egrets, godwits, and curlews. A lone osprey circled above, while a pair of aggressive Forster's terns dove for silvery baitfish. The canoe had brought us into a marine environment others couldn't reach. There really isn't one ultimate watercraft for all angling situations, but the canoe's traditional design comes close to perfection for exploring the Pacific coastline's protected waters.

As with any piece of equipment, the more techniques you're able to execute when paddling a canoe, the better the results at day's end. It's a matter of maximizing the boat's strengths and staying safely within the parameters of its design.

I recognize there are pros and cons to all designs, but I believe the canoe's positive features far outweigh its negatives. Its strength lies in its simplicity. Long, graceful lines are a key to the canoe's functionality. The subtle sweep from front to back facilitates efficient movement with little drag. This sleek craft can navigate the narrowest of waterways. Its ability to float in mere inches of water allows access where other craft can't go. A canoe is small enough and light enough to launch just about anywhere you please. In most cases, it can be lifted by a single person, and car-topping a canoe makes life on the road painless.

There are a number of canoe models to choose from, depending on the water you plan to fish. The basic categories include recreational, wilderness-tripping, and racing-style hulls. Three qualities to look for in a boat's design are load-carrying capacity, stability, and motoring or paddling mechanics.

We've come a long way in the materials used in canoe construction. The list now includes wood, aluminum, fiberglass, Royalex, Kevlar, Carbonlite, and various foam-core synthetics. All contribute to the hull's durability, weight, and insulating properties. For saltwater explorations,

I believe the synthetic hulls are most appropriate.

Fly fishers should consider models with a broader beam and a slightly flat-bottomed hull. In fact, shallow-V designs offer the best all-around stability. They tend to cut into a rolling, choppy surface. Flat-bottomed designs will rock away from any point of disturbance, creating maximum tipping effect. Recreational hulls are the most versatile in this regard. They're generally fourteen to sixteen feet in length. Their weight can vary from fifty-eight to eighty-five pounds, depending on the materials used. Wilderness-tripping designs are geared for extended backcountry use, especially for the exploration of large lakes. They are best-suited for fly fishing in expansive bay habitats. Longer hulls are faster and easier to paddle.

One of the drawbacks to fishing from canoes is their susceptibility to wind. Before heading into any coastal waters, be acutely aware of wind patterns that can make paddling and holding a straight course more difficult. When in doubt, don't go out!

In most cases, paddles are your means of locomotion. They come in a variety of sizes, weights, and designs. Optimal paddle length is a function of shaft length. The shaft runs from top of the grip to the top of the blade. To find a straight-shaft paddle that is the right length for you, sit or kneel in a canoe with your back straight. Place the grip of the paddle on the floor of the canoe and hold the paddle vertically in front of you. The point where the shaft meets the blade should be just about nose height. This measurement gives you a long enough paddle to reach the water comfortably. Bent-shaft paddles will be about six inches shorter than straight-shaft paddles. Straight-shaft designs are the easiest for beginners. Bent-shaft paddles were developed by marathon canoeists. While you can do the same strokes with a bent-shaft paddle that you can do with a straight-shaft paddle, the bent-shaft paddle works best when you need to go in a more-or-less straight line for long distances.

With a motor mount and trolling motor, you can easily convert your canoe from hand-powered to battery-powered in a matter of seconds. Today's trolling motors are lightweight, quiet, and powerful. Saltwater versions are now available. Since you could find yourself working against a strong current, consider using a motor rated at 30-pounds thrust or more.

For holding your position against the current or slowing your descent down an estuary, a simple river-style anchor might be the answer. In most cases, a 10-pound or 12-pound anchor will be more than sufficient to get the job done. The three short modified wings of a river anchor hold exceptionally well in an estuary's sandy floor. In currents take care not to drag an anchor, accidentally or on purpose. A hang-up could swamp the boat. A quick release knot and an easily reachable knife are good safety precautions when using anchors in moving water.

Using a canoe for fly fishing requires a bit of forethought. Haphazard storage of gear usually results in a very long day with little or no angling success. I try to eliminate noise from items rattling across the boat's floor. I use soft containers to hold my terminal tackle, secured by clips on the wall of the canoe or hanging underneath the bow and stern seats. Hard plastic containers such as battery boxes rest on pieces of closed-cell foam. When I'm fishing solo, I store my rod in a C-clamp holder perched on the center thwart. The cradle of the clamp is set so the rod rests parallel to the boat. To land and release my catch, I use a Boga Grip secured by a quick-release ring attached to the center thwart. Its handle lies on a bed of foam, too. Everything is within easy reach from my piloting position.

Trolling motors can increase your range and safety.
PHOTOGRAPH BY GLENN KISHI

A stripping basket can be a handy tool to hold loose line in a canoe. An alternative is to use two bungee cords stretched across the canoe to support a draped mesh cloth that catches the unruly coils of line while you're retrieving your fly.

Casting from a canoe doesn't have to be an uncomfortable experience. The best position for balancing and controlling the craft, one that guarantees a low center of gravity in open water, also is a good one for casting. A kneeling position close to the center of the canoe allows you to brace your knees against the walls of the boat or your thighs under the center thwart. It gives you superior control of the craft in rough water and is especially good while executing long casts.

If you stand in the craft to cast, however, you definitely will find it feels unstable. When I'm estuary fishing, if I really feel the need to stand, I'll simply beach the canoe and wade on a sandbar next to it. And even

Kneeling in a central position creates more stability and helps line control.
PHOTOGRAPH BY KEN HANLEY

though you'll be using the canoe in fairly calm waters, always be alert and always carry the same safety essentials listed at the end of the preceding chapter on kayaks.

It doesn't matter if you cast from the canoe or simply use the boat as a taxi. Don't miss the opportunity to explore the West Coast's estuaries and harbors with this time-proven design.

SKIFFS ARE SYNONYMOUS with the saltwater environment. They're also a wonderfully adaptable craft. Although the term "skiff" can mean anything from a small, light sailing ship to a light rowboat, for our purposes it refers to a small motorized craft. The boating industry categorizes skiffs as boats ranging in size from eleven to twenty-three feet in overall length. Craft in the fourteen-foot to twenty-foot range seem to be the most popular among inshore and nearshore anglers. These also offer fly fishers significant safety features and angling options. But larger skiffs are just fine if you prefer one.

Hard hulls are constructed from wood, fiberglass, and/or metal. Numerous designs have incorporated a foam core for insulation and extra flotation. Inflatables, known as RIBs (Rigid Inflatable Boats), offer another option. These are hybrid designs sporting fiberglass floorboards and hulls coupled with Hypalon-neoprene flotation tubes. Today's market

Captain Bill Matthews and the author head out for a day's fishing.
PHOTOGRAPH BY GLENN KISHI

presents myriad options. I still have a soft spot in my heart for traditional wooden lapstrake designs.

Each of the hull materials mentioned has its own unique qualities. You should consult the manufacturers to understand the strengths and weaknesses of each kind of material. For example, fiberglass weighs substantially more than aluminum, yet aluminum requires more maintenance than fiberglass. Wood generally weighs less than aluminum, but also requires the most maintenance of all hull materials. The kind of hull you choose depends on your own personality and angling needs.

Power for these vessels typically comes from an outboard engine. Don't make the mistake of overpowering your boat. Each craft has a power-rating standard set by the United States Coast Guard. An industry rule of thumb targets 80 percent of this rated capacity as ideal for all-around performance. You can operate smaller skiffs with as little as a 10-horsepower motor. Most twenty-foot skiffs work well within the

Tom Malech gives a stripping bucket a try.
PHOTOGRAPH BY KEN HANLEY

range of a 150-horsepower engine. You simply need a motor that will allow you to control the boat under all conditions.

Skiffs allow you to move from place to place rapidly, if necessary, and to move about easily within the craft. They have room for storage and can take anglers on long-range fishing expeditions. Line snags and tangles abound in most skiffs, however. You can't eliminate all the obstructions that cause them, but you can reduce the prospective trouble zones.

It takes an astute skipper to prepare a boat to become fly-line friendly. Check cleats, oarlocks, fuel tanks, batteries, antennae, and the anchor system. This is just a partial listing—it can seem as if an endless array of traps await your fly line, so keep everything stowed. Rod racks and tackle bags should be part of your storage system. Use a tarp or damp towel to cover obstructions, creating slick zones over which your line can travel. If you don't have retractable cleats, try using small plastic containers to cover them. Do what you can to reduce sharp edges. And be sure to isolate any potential contaminants such as oil and gas from coming in contact with your line.

Two effective tools for fly-line management are line buckets or stripping baskets. I'm not a big fan of "waist" baskets. I prefer to work from a bucket, instead. I can simply move the container anywhere I need at a moment's notice. Buckets offer a larger area for line storage and allow you to strip with a full arm pull, while baskets restrict you to shorter arm movements. Keeping a small amount of water in the bucket container also helps relax your line and reduces tangles. I've worked with simple five-gallon paint buckets and custom commercial fly-line tamers. They both increase the level of efficiency and enjoyment. The ultimate situation is to provide a bucket or basket for each angler on board.

If you don't favor either of these line containers, carry a piece of marine-grade carpet about three feet square and strip your line onto that. It's easy to keep it clean of debris and contaminants. The carpet can also double as a safety surface on which an angler can stand.

Built-in or portable live wells are priceless. So is a good selection of flies.
PHOTOGRAPH BY GLENN KISHI

The extra carrying capacity of skiffs means that you can haul more equipment, but much of that equipment can serve more than one purpose. For example, ice chests in the 60-quart and 90-plus-quart sizes can be used as seating and platforms on which to stand.

They also can be converted into live wells by using portable aerators, as can a wide variety of utility buckets. There are aerator units that run on a pair of D-cell alkaline batteries and conversion kits that tap into the skiff's twelve-volt system. Live wells thus needn't be large or expensive items. Having live bait to attract or hold gamefish within casting range is a luxury anyone can enjoy. If you'd prefer a live well designed for the purpose, however, consider rotomolded polyethylene tanks that are built for large skiffs.

Trolling motors provide control and maneuverability for working along kelp lines or staying over reef structure. Saltwater-specific motors boast stainless steel or composite shafts, corrosion-resistant alloy components, plus sealed wiring and electrical systems. Boating in the marine environment, you're sure to experience choppy seas, strong currents, and swells, and trolling motors need to have the capacity to handle these conditions. Use a motor that provides a minimum of thirty-six pounds thrust. There are models that can provide up to seventy-five pounds of thrust. In any case, use the longest shaft available. Should you get a bow mount or transom model? Trolling motors in fact steer better with when they're pulling the boat. But don't let that stop you from a transom-tiller option.

Electronics help reveal structure, schooling bait, and much more.
PHOTOGRAPH BY GLENN KISHI

Drogues, commonly referred to as drift socks, are another way to increase boat control. These are basically chutes constructed of various lightweight materials such as vinyl and ripstop nylon. A tether twenty-five to thirty feet long secures the chute to your boat. Employed as drag, the drogue's cone creates resistance to both current and wind effects on your skiff. The sock can be employed from any position on the skiff to maintain a slower drift. These adjustable sea anchors come in a variety of sizes—hoop diameter is the most significant dimension. In general, boats under seventeen feet can use a seventeen-inch-diameter sock. Larger skiffs will need chutes varying in diameter from twenty to thirty inches.

No matter how much equipment you carry in your skiff, there's no substitute for learning the basic skills of reading water and understanding nature's myriad clues that tell you where to find fish. Still, there are aids to that end that have become indispensable. Sonar displays have become standard equipment for interpreting structure, depth, and bait movement. Used properly, they can eliminate vast areas of unproductive water. It's amazing to see the levels of sophistication now built into this tool. You'll find models with features such as integrated Loran and GPS, surface water temperature detection, side-scanning, boat speed and distance computation, 3-D imaging, and split-screen capabilities.

There's one last item that is almost as valuable, but extremely low-tech: a set of marker buoys. Often you need to mark the X on the treasure map of your day's fishing. Seasoned skippers frequently deploy floats to assist them in tracing drift routes and pinpointing specific structure. You might also use them to show where schooling activity was encountered. Buy a set or make a set. Carry a set. You won't be disappointed that you did. Four to six plastic milk jugs, each tied to eighty feet of cord and a five-ounce lead weight will do the trick just fine.

Finally there are some items you should always carry in your skiff to keep you safe while boating Big Blue and to get you safely home. Some

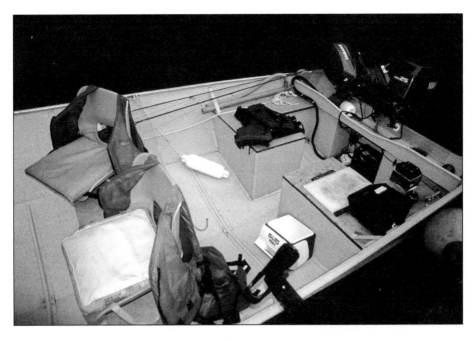

are required by the United States Coast Guard. Check with state laws for any additional items required. Miscellaneous additional recommendations also come from a variety of boating associations.

1. Personal flotation device: one life vest per person
2. Fire extinguisher: one B-1, any type, is required on boats with enclosed engine compartments (but not on outboards), boats with enclosed living spaces, and boats with permanent fuel tanks. B-1 extinguishers are capable of extinguish flammable liquids, including gasoline, oil, kerosene, diesel fuel, alcohol, tar, paint, and lacquer.
3. Visual distress signals: a minimum of three day-use and three night-use or three day/night combinations. Pyrotechnic and nonpyrotechnic options are acceptable.
4. Safety horn or whistle.
5. Navigation lights.
6. First-aid and emergency kits.
7. Extra clothing, food, and water.
8. Paddle(s).
9. Tool kit.
10. Spare propeller and engine parts.
11. Anchor.
12. Charts and a compass.
13. VHF radio.

Know the limits of your gear before you head out. Stay in calm conditions.
PHOTOGRAPH BY GLENN KISHI

I'M OFTEN ASKED ABOUT THE IDEA of fishing from a float tube in California coastal waters. I hear many first-hand accounts of saltwater tubers and their successes, as well as their concerns. I've also witnessed fly fishers working from tubes in environments ranging from kelp beds and open shores to jetties and quiet harbors, and I have some definite opinions about the subject.

First, let me emphasize—strongly emphasize, in fact—that I don't endorse float tubes and pontoon boats for general saltwater use. When fishing in a marine environment, you are subject to greater risk when using these watercraft than when fishing from a kayak, canoe, skiff, or even afoot. But I also know there are people using these devices for fly fishing salt water along the Pacific coastline, and there are more who may be tempted to do so. You need to know the risk involved before you can wisely accept any challenge. I'm not trying to dictate your adventure. I'm simply trying to present all the factors involved. Think before you float. And if you decide the risks aren't worth taking, you'll arrive the easy way at a conclusion that others have had to reach the hard way.

Everyone's first reaction is to worry about a shark attack. Although this is a potential hazard, I've yet to see a confirmed report of such an encounter. There are far more likely dangers for you to acknowledge: tidal influence, current strength, wave structure and timing, surface and subsurface debris, a tube's low visible profile, and its limited maneuvering capabilities. If what follows does not succeed in discouraging you, and float tubing in the salt is an activity that you feel you must explore, please pay attention to all of these variables, all the time.

The saltwater environment is inextricably tied to tidal influence. Some places are affected more dramatically than others. Take Alaska, for example, where tides can rise or drop twenty feet or more in a single phase. California waters fluctuate an average of three to six feet, but swings of seven feet or more occur, depending on the season. That is a lot of moving water, and the energy behind it is immense. In a tube, it doesn't take much to feel the true power of the sea.

The greater the difference between high and low tides, the stronger the effects will be on you and your watercraft. If you are indeed set on using a float tube, you need a clear picture of the tidal patterns at your destination at the time that you'll be fishing. Do your homework. Check the lunar cycle first. The new and full phases of the moon produce the most dramatic swings in the tide.

As the tide rises or drops, you'll be faced with new challenges. Entry and exit sites will change, and in some cases, what was an easy place to put in will be completely out of the question as a way out. Also keep in mind that a tide doesn't rise or fall gradually and steadily. It surges. These short, intense surges can easily overwhelm unsuspecting tubers.

Though tides are perpetually in flux, currents are a constant presence. Their intensity may vary at times, but their effect is uniform. All saltwater anglers should learn to interpret the water around them. Rip lines and current seams affect float tubes, as well as fish. Currents are typically associated with jetty habitats, but they also exist around tapering points and deepwater edges. Currents are common in open water, as well. The combined movement of tide and current can create complex conditions that you may not be able to cope with in a float tube.

Most of the waves we see are created by the force of winds offshore. The stronger the wind, the longer it blows, the greater the wave's size and strength. Conditions at your fishing destination thus can be affected by weather far out at sea. A wave builds in height and power over a shallow bottom, so you're likely to find calmer conditions in deeper water—which will also be farther away from the safety of shore. The time between waves is known as an interval. A series of intervals is known as a set. Be aware of the rhythm of waves. Sets can and do change during a tidal surge.

Debris is inevitable in the marine environment: kelp, seaweed, driftwood, and other debris, plus various flotsam of all kinds added by freshwater flows from shore. Anytime you're around currents or waves, be alert. On the surface, smaller items are tough to see among the waves and swells. Subsurface, it's easy to become entangled in kelp or discarded rope, or run into a sunken log.

Float tubes ride low to the surface. Other boaters, including other tubers, have a hard time seeing you from a safe distance. This problem is compounded by low light or fog, the very conditions whose effect on fishing prospects may tempt you to venture out. Take a cue from the diving community. They use a simple system to announce their presence. On a small, inflatable platform, often just a basic inner tube, they fly a high-visibility flag secured to a long fiberglass pole. It works. Visit a dive shop, adapt the equipment for use on your float tube, and adopt the practice.

Also, the fact that tubes are incredibly slow should be an area of concern for everyone. You can't outrun a wave. You can't outrun a swift current, or the debris trapped in that flow. You certainly can't outrun a larger vessel bearing down on you.

An inflatable pontoon craft is a bit more maneuverable than a tube, but still generally slower than any hard-hull craft. I view pontoons as a compromise in saltwater conditions. Why not just reap the benefits and safety of a hard-hull design? Kayaks, canoes, and skiffs will provide a much greater margin of safety. I'd confine my use of float tubes and pontoons to protected backwaters. It's impossible to eliminate all the safety concerns with any watercraft, but you will be in an environment that better suits your choice of vessel.

If you're still inclined to venture into salt water in a float tube, take heed of the following cautionary tale, which is true.

The fly fisher had launched his float tube from a comfortable sandbar. It was during a low, slack tide, and the incoming flood was yet to build in the quiet harbor. As the angler drifted away from the shallows, he felt a steady current begin to dictate the path of his craft. Taking advantage of the current's momentum, he directed his tube toward the surface seam that was parallel to the nearby jetty. In a matter of moments, he was casting toward the breakwater's wall, intently working the streamer to imitate a disoriented baitfish.

Keeping his legs in constant motion and working to hold his position in the current, he hadn't noticed the subtle change in the tide. About twenty minutes had elapsed. He was becoming fatigued. And he hadn't anticipated the tidal surge. In what seemed an instant, the power of the tide had taken complete command of his float tube, slamming him against the jetty. He was pinned to the structure, and the combination of tide, current, and wave action grated his tube against a razor-sharp mussel bed and abrasive cement blocks. Though he tried to find secure footing, his fins wouldn't allow a safe purchase. He was trapped, exhausted, and at the mercy of nature's uncaring forces.

But the surge subsided, and after a few minutes, the float tuber was able to regain his composure. Still, it took the aid of a few bystanders to assist him safely ashore. The bottom of his craft was shredded. His hands were covered with contusions and small cuts. He was fortunate. Another surge was imminent, and his equipment clearly wasn't capable of handling such conditions.

You can't underestimate the power of the marine environment or the limitations of your equipment and skills. I've stressed the need for carrying safety and emergency gear in other forms of watercraft. That need rises exponentially if you're going to venture into even protected Pacific waters in a float tube or pontoon boat. Make sure you have and know how to use all of the following.

1. Personal flotation device (life vest).
2. Neoprene waders.
3. Knife (a fixed, serrated single blade).
4. Extra fins or a small paddle.
5. Tow rope with a throw bag (a minimum of fifty feet of ⅜-inch polypro or Spectra rope).
6. Diver's flag secured to a long fiberglass pole.
7. Hand-held VHF radio—not a walkie-talkie. A VHF radio allows you to communicate with other boats and the Coast Guard in emergencies.
8. Safety whistle (all-weather model). These high-impact plastic whistles work even when wet, unlike the classic coach's whistle with the "pea" inside. One model even works underwater.

MOST OF THE FLIES LISTED HERE are commercially available through fly shops and mail-order catalogs. A few are custom designs. As a collection, they outfit a fly fisher for estuary, bay, and beach adventures. I've included the target species for each fly and pointed out the preferred habitat for using each pattern. Where appropriate, the bait being imitated is also listed. These patterns are in alphabetical order.

ALF BAITFISH (created by Bill and Kate Howe)

Hook: Size 2 to 3/0 (sample: Gamakatsu Trey Combs Saltwater).
Thread: White 6/0 for small hooks, Nymo "A" for large hooks.
Belly: Polar bear Super Hair, Pearl Flashabou, silver holographic Angel Hair.
Lateral Line: Silver holographic Mylar.
Top Line: Polar bear Super Hair, Olive-dyed pearl Flashabou.
Topping: Pheasant tail Angel Hair.
Cheeks: Red FisHair.
Head: Tying thread, colored on top with a brown marker.
Eyes: Prismatic stick-on, silver with black pupils.
  (Soft Body or epoxy is used to coat head and eyes.)
Target species: Tuna, salmon, corvina, barracuda, striped bass, sand bass, rockfish, mackerel.
Habitat use: Open bays, estuaries, harbors, rocky shores, kelp beds, beaches.
Bait imitated: Anchovies, herring, sardines, mackerel, sand lances, candlefish.

CDC SHRIMP (created by Michael Andersen)

Hook: Size 4 to 8 (sample: Daiichi 2059, TMC 7989).
Thread: Match body color, 6/0 standard, Kevlar, or Flymaster Plus.
Antennae: Grizzly hackle, stripped.
Mouthpart: Teal flank fibers.
Eyes: Burned 10-pound test mono.
Shellback: Clear or speckled/mottled synthetic (Thin Skin, Shimazaki, Scud Back).
Body: Golden olive SLF dubbing, (variations: fluorescent pink, orange, rust brown, white, or tan).
Legs: Pale yellow or light dun CDC feather, folded over back.
Ribbing: 6-pound monofilament or tying thread.
Head: Tying thread.
Target species: Salmon.
Habitat use: Estuaries, kelp beds.
Bait imitated: Krill and euphausiid shrimp.

Color photographs of flies follow page 88.

CLOUSER MINNOW (created by Bob Clouser)

Hook: Size 4 to 1/0 (sample: TMC 811S, Mustad 3407, Daiichi 2546).
Thread: White or olive 6/0 standard, Kevlar, or Flymaster Plus.
Eyes: Medium nontoxic barbells, painted red with black pupils, tied on top of shank.
Tail: White bucktail (optional).
Belly: White bucktail atop the shank. (Fly rides point-up.)
Wing: Olive bucktail on the bottom of the shank with olive Krystal Flash accent (variations: white/chartreuse, white/green, white/brown, or yellow/brown).
Head: Tying thread.
Target species: Rockfish, flatfish, striped bass, sand bass, barracuda, white seabass, tuna, mackerel.
Habitat use: Open bays, estuaries, harbors, kelp beds, rocky shores, beaches.
Bait imitated: Pinhead anchovies, sand lances, sardines, candlefish, and herring.

DEEP CANDY BENDBACK (created by Bob Popovics)

Hook: Size 1/0 (sample: Mustad 34011).
Thread: White 3/0 monocord or single-strand floss.
Weight: Silver nontoxic medium or large conehead, silver.
Wing: Ultra Hair (or equivalent), polar white, bottom half, with sparse pearlescent Krystal Flash accent. Olive (or brown), top half of wing.
Lateral Line: Prismatic tape.
Head: Tying thread and five-minute epoxy.
Eyes: Stick-on eyes, silver with black pupils.
Target species: Sand bass, flatfish, rockfish, corvina.
Habitat use: Estuaries, harbors, kelp beds.
Bait imitated: Pinhead anchovies, sand lances, candlefish.

DEER HAIR SHRIMP (created by Jack Horner)

Hook: Size 4 (sample: TMC 7999, Daiichi 2441, Mustad 36890).
Thread: Black 6/0 standard, Kevlar, or Flymaster Plus.
Weight: Medium nontoxic round wire, wrapped.
Tail: Natural bucktail.
Shellback: Natural bucktail.
Body: Oval silver tinsel, spiral wrapped.
Hackle: Grizzly, palmered over the body before the shellback is pulled over.
Head: Tying thread.
Eyes: Painted (optional), white with black pupils.
Target species: Salmon.
Habitat use: Estuaries and harbors.
Bait imitated: Various tidal shrimp.

DIAMOND SHRIMP (created by Ken Hanley)

Hook: Size 5 to 7 (sample: Daiichi 2052, TMC 7989).
Thread: White or pink 6/0 standard or single-strand floss.
Antennae: A few strands of pearlescent Krystal Flash and gold Flashabou.
Skirt: White or pink rabbit fur, applied in a dubbing loop.
Body: Pearl, gold, or fluorescent shrimp-pink diamond braid.
Head: Tying thread.
Target species: Salmon, smelt.
Habitat use: Estuaries, kelp beds.
Bait imitated: Euphausiid shrimp and krill.

FATAL ATTRACTION (created by Dan Blanton)

Hook: Size 2 to 4 (sample: TMC 7989, 7999, Daiichi 2421, Mustad 36890).
Thread: Green 6/0 standard.
Tail: Silver Flashabou.
Body: Silver diamond braid.
Underwing: Yellow bucktail, sparse, with pearl blue and peacock accent flashes.
Collar: Yellow saddle hackle.
Overwing: Peacock herl.
Eyes: Medium bead chain.
Head: Tying thread.
Target species: Salmon, mackerel.
Habitat use: Kelp beds, estuaries.
Bait imitated: Generic attractor.

FLASHTAIL WHISTLER (created by Dan Blanton)

Hook: Size 1/0 to 3/0 (sample: Mustad 9175, TMC 800S).
Thread: Red, Nymo "A" or equivalent.
Weight: Nontoxic .030-inch round wire, wrapped, ten turns.
Eyes: Large silver bead chain.
Flashtail: Silver Flashabou.
Body: White bucktail, pearl accent flash, Grizzly saddle hackle.
Collar: Red chenille.
Hackle: Grizzly saddle hackle.
Target species: Striped bass, sharks, white seabass.
Habitat use: Open bays, kelp beds, harbors.
Bait imitated: Generic attractor (color variations: red hackle and white body, all-black).

GOLD BUCCANEER (created by Ken Hanley)

Hook: Size 2 to 1/0 (sample: TMC 811S, TMC 8089NP).
Thread: Fluorescent yellow floss and yellow or orange 6/0 standard, Kevlar, or Flymaster Plus.
Tail and Antennae: White bucktail.
Tip: Fluorescent yellow floss.
Eyes: Large nontoxic barbells or bead chain.
Wing: Peacock Krystal Flash and gold Flashabou.
Body: (change to yellow standard tying thread) yellow Lite Brite, applied in a dubbing loop.
Collar: Large, webby saddle hackle, 1 or 2 yellow, 1 orange.
Head: Tying thread.
Target species: Rockfish, sand bass, flatfish.
Habitat use: Rocky shores, estuaries, harbors, kelp beds.
Bait imitated: Large shrimp (i.e. ghost shrimp). Also a generic attractor.

GREEN COMET

Hook: Size 2 to 8 (sample: TMC 7989, 7999, Daiichi 2441, Mustad 36890).
Thread: Chartreuse or fluorescent green 6/0 standard or Flymaster Plus.
Tail: Chartreuse bucktail.
Body: Silver Mylar.
Ribbing: Silver oval tinsel.
Collar: Chartreuse saddle hackle.
Eyes: Large bead-chain.
Head: Tying thread.
Target species: Salmon.
Habitat use: Estuaries, kelp beds.
Bait imitated: Generic attractor.

JAY'S GRASS SHRIMP (created by Jay Murakoshi)

Hook: Size 4 (sample: Daiichi 2546, Mustad 3407).
Thread: Gray or white 6/0 standard or 3/0 monocord.
Eyes: Plastic nymph eyes, medium.
Antennae: Grizzly stems, stripped.
Tail and shellback: Gray bucktail.
Body: Pearl blue Lite Brite, picked out.
Head: Tying thread.
Target species: Rockfish, surfperch, flatfish, sand bass.
Habitat use: Beaches, estuaries, harbors.
Bait imitated: Grass shrimp and others.

JENSEN FOAM SLIDER (created by Milt Jensen)

Hook: Size 2 (sample: TMC 9394, Daiichi 2460).
Thread: White 3/0 monocord.
Tail: White or gray marabou, with sparse pearl Krystal Flash accent.
Body: Foam strip cut to shape. Pearl or silver Mylar tubing as cover. Marking pens are used to create accent marks and color variations.
Eyes: Stick-on plastic eyes.
Weed guard: light wire (optional).
Head: Tying thread.
Target species: Salmon and rockfish.
Habitat use: Estuaries.
Bait imitated: Anchovies, herring, sand lances, candlefish.

LABYRINTH CRAB (created by Ken Hanley)

Hook: Size 2 to 1/0 (sample: TMC 800S, Mustad 3407, Daiichi 2546).
Thread: Match body color, 6/0 standard, Kevlar, or Flymaster Plus.
Weight: Medium nontoxic round wire, wrapped.
Butt: Fluorescent orange chenille, small ball at midshank.
Claws: Pheasant tail on bottom, grizzly hackle tips on top.
Rear Hackle: Grizzly.
Body: Opossum, (variations: bleached, tan, red, purple, or brown).
Collar: Any soft hackle.
Head: Tying thread.
Target species: Rockfish, sand bass, striped bass.
Habitat use: Rocky shores, estuaries, harbors.
Bait imitated: Various rock, shore, and porcelain crabs.

LEFTY'S DECEIVER (created by Lefty Kreh)

Hook: Size 2 to 3/0 (sample: TMC 800S, 811S).
Thread: White 3/0 monocord or single-strand floss.
Tail: Six white saddle hackles, with 6 to 12 strands of pearl Krystal Flash per side as accents.
Body: Silver flat tinsel.
Wing: Blue bucktail on top, white below (variations: green/white, red/white, olive/white, red/yellow, or all-white).
Topping: Peacock herl, a few strands.
Hackle Wing: One grizzly hackle per side.
Throat: Red Krystal Flash.
Head: Tying thread painted blue or black.
Eyes: Small plastic doll eyes or painted eyes, white with black pupils.
Target species: White seabass, sharks, flatfish, rockfish.
Habitat use: Open bays, estuaries, harbors, kelp beds, beaches.
Bait imitated: Anchovies, sardines, herring, sand lances, candlefish.

MICRO SHRIMP (created by Jay Murakoshi)

Hook: Size 6 (sample: Daiichi 2546, Mustad 3407).
Thread: Red 6/0 standard, Kevlar, or Flymaster Plus.
Tail: Red bucktail.
Shellback: Red bucktail.
Body: Silver diamond braid.
Head: Tying thread.
Target species: Surfperch.
Habitat use: Beaches.
Bait imitated: Generic small shrimp.

NEAR 'NUFF SCULPIN (created by Dave Whitlock)

Hook: Size 4 to 6 (sample: TMC 5263).
Thread: Green or tan, match body color, 6/0 standard.
Tail: Olive or tan grizzly hen hackle tips with a sparse pearl Krystal Flash accent.
Ribbing: Olive or tan thread.
Body: Olive or tan standard dubbing.
Hackle: Olive or tan soft grizzly hackle, palmered.
Eyes/Weight: Medium nontoxic barbell eyes, painted black with white pupils.
Head: Dubbing.
Target species: Surfperch.
Habitat use: Beaches.
Bait imitated: Small sculpins and crustaceans, generic attractor.

PEARL YETI (created by Ken Hanley)

Hook: Size 2 to 5 (sample: TMC 7989, Daiichi 2059).
Thread: White 6/0 standard or single-strand floss.
Tag: Fluorescent green floss.
Butt: Tying thread.
Tail: White polypropylene yarn.
Body: Pearl blue Lite Brite, applied in a dubbing loop.
Collar: Teal flank.
Wing: White calf tail.
Head: Tying thread.
Target species: Bonito, mackerel, smelt, salmon.
Habitat use: Estuaries, harbors.
Bait imitated: Young baitfish.

PINK POLLYWOG (created by Dec Hogan)

Hook: Size 2 (sample: Daiichi 2720, TMC 8089NP).
Thread: Fluorescent pink 3/0 monocord.
Tail: Fluorescent pink marabou with pearl Krystal Flash accent.
Body: Fluorescent pink deer hair.
Head: Tying thread.
Target species: Salmon.
Habitat use: Estuaries.
Bait imitated: Generic attractor.

RABBIT-STRIP FLY

Hook: Size 2 to 1/0 (sample: Gamakatsu Trey Combs, TMC 800S, Daiichi 2546, Mustad 3407).
Thread: Brown, or match body color (variations; all-white, all-black, white/red, or all-chartreuse), 6/0 standard, Kevlar, or Flymaster Plus.
Tail: Brown rabbit Zonker strip.
Skirt: Brown cross-cut rabbit strip, wrapped.
Eyes/Weight: Medium or large nontoxic barbells.
Head: Brown Buggy Nymph dubbing.
Target species: Rockfish, flatfish, sand bass, calico bass, sharks.
Habitat use: Kelp beds, rocky shores, estuaries, harbors.
Bait imitated: Generic attractor.

RUSTY SQUIRREL CLOUSER

(variation of Bob Clouser's Minnow, by Jay Murakoshi)

Hook: Size 4 to 6 (sample: Daiichi 2546, Mustad 3407, TMC 800S).
Thread: Red 6/0 standard, Kevlar, or Flymaster Plus.
Tail: Natural or brown squirrel tail.
Body: Gold diamond braid.
Eyes/Weight: Medium or large nontoxic barbells.
Belly: Squirrel on top of the shank.
Wing: Squirrel on the bottom of the shank, with rainbow or pearl Krystal Flash accent.
Head: Tying thread.
Target species: Surfperch.
Habitat use: Beaches.
Bait imitated: Generic attractor.

SALMON WAKER (created by Larry Dahlberg)

Hook: Size 2 (sample: Daiichi 2720, TMC 8089NP).
Thread: Green 3/0 monocord.
Tail: Green rabbit Zonker strip with green Flashabou.
Body: Green cross-cut rabbit strip, a few wraps.
Collar: Fluorescent green deer hair.
Head: Fluorescent green deer hair, trimmed to shape.
Target species: Salmon.
Habitat use: Estuaries.
Bait imitated: Generic attractor.

SEA ARROW SQUID (created by Dan Blanton)

Hook: Size 2/0 to 4/0 (sample: Eagle Claw 66-SS).
Thread: White, Nymo "A" or equivalent.
Tip: Gold Mylar.
Butt: Large white chenille wrapped into a ball.
Tail: Eight white saddle hackles 3 inches long, tied in as a wing. Add one white hackle 5 inches long to each side. Add a few 3-inch strands of coarse purple bucktail and purple Krystal Flash to each side.
Eyes: Amber 8-mm glass eyes.
Topping and Throat: Fill the gap between the eyes with white marabou.
Body: Build the base with floss or cotton thread. Taper it toward the hook eye. Wrap with white medium chenille. Leave room near the hook eye to add two tufts of calf tail as a horizontal posterior fin.
Target species: Rockfish, calico bass, sharks, white seabass, tuna.
Habitat use: Open bays, kelp beds, harbors.
Bait imitated: Opalescent squid.

SEA HABIT BUCKTAIL (created by Trey Combs)

Hook: Size 1/0 to 3/0 (sample: Gamakatsu Trey Combs Saltwater).
Thread: White single-strand floss.
Tail: Pearl rainbow Spectra Mylar Motion tinsel.
Underbody: White bucktail, pearl Spectra Mylar Motion tinsel, white FisHair.
Shoulders: Pearl Krystal Flash, gray ghost Krystal Flash.
Midback: Gray ghost Krystal Flash, gray FisHair, gray ghost Krystal Flash, gray bucktail, gray ghost Krystal Flash.
Cheeks: Silver Flashabou.
Topping: Peacock herl.
Head: Pearl Mylar tube, top colored with Scribbles T-shirt paint, Nightstar color, then coated with epoxy.
Eyes: Stick-on pearlescent eyes with black pupils.
Target species: Tuna, striped bass, rockfish, salmon.
Habitat use: Open bays, kelp beds, harbors.
Bait imitated: Anchovies, sardines, herring.

SOCKEYE BOSS (created by Rich Culver)

Hook: Size 4 to 8 (sample: TMC 7999, 7989, Daiichi 2059).
Thread: Red or burgundy 6/0 standard, Kevlar, or Flymaster Plus.
Tail: Black squirrel tail.
Body: Medium black Larva Lace.
Hackle: Chartreuse saddle hackle.
Eyes/Weight: Medium bead chain.
Head: Tying thread.
Target species: Salmon.
Habitat use: Estuaries.
Bait imitated: Generic attractor.

SOCKEYE SPECIAL

Hook: Size 6 to 8 (sample: TMC 7999, 7989, Daiichi 2059).
Thread: Black 6/0 standard, Kevlar, or Flymaster Plus.
Wing: Black deer hair.
Throat: Orange deer hair.
Head: Tying thread.
Target species: Salmon.
Habitat use: Estuaries.
Bait imitated: Generic attractor.

SORCERER'S TOUCH (created by Ken Hanley)

Hook: Size 2 to 4 (sample: Daiichi 2059, TMC 7989, 7999).
Thread: Black 6/0 standard, Kevlar, or Flymaster Plus.
Tag: Silver tinsel.
Tail: Silver-gray Antron.
Body: Silver-gray Antron, wrapped.
Wing: Silver-gray Antron spikes, tied Aztec-style.
Accent Wing: Green Antron with blue squirrel tail.
Throat: Gray marabou.
Hackle: Light blue saddle hackle (additional teal flank optional).
Head: Gray standard dubbing.
Target species: Salmon.
Habitat use: Estuaries, kelp beds.
Bait imitated: Generic attractor.

SURF GRUB (created by Ken Hanley)

Hook: Size 10 to 6 (sample: TMC 8089NP).
Thread: Olive 6/0 standard, Kevlar, or Flymaster Plus.
Eyes: Medium or large nontoxic barbells.
Tail: Spooled Antron, equal lengths of gray, olive, and orange, veiled with tan and gray marabou.
Body: Olive Antron, twisted and wrapped.
Head: Medium hot pink or red-orange chenille.
Target species: Surfperch.
Habitat use: Beaches.
Bait imitated: Generic attractor, Pacific mole crab roe.

SURFPERCHER RED (created by John Shewey)

Hook: Size 2 to 4 (sample: Mustad 3407).
Thread: Red 6/0 standard, Kevlar, or Flymaster Plus.
Tail: Yellow or red marabou tips.
Body: Red or gold diamond braid.
Wing: Red marabou with sparse red Krystal Flash accent.
Eyes/Weight: Large bead chain.
Head: Tying thread.
Target species: Surfperch.
Habitat use: Beaches.
Bait imitated: Generic attractor, Pacific mole crab roe.

TRES GENERATION POPPER (created by Dale Hightower)

Hook: Size 1/0 to 4/0 (Owner 5230 RE, plated).
Thread: White 3/0 monocord or single-strand floss.
Tail: White neck hackles, 3 per side, splayed, plus the frayed ends of the body tubing.
Undercollar: Masking tape built up just behind the hook's eye, or 28-gauge shotgun wad.
Body: Large pearl Mylar tubing, marking pens used to make accent marks and color variations. Coated with two-part thirty-minute epoxy and rotated.
Eyes: Stick-on plastic, white hologram with black pupils.
Head: Tying thread.
Target species: Tuna, striped bass.
Habitat use: Open bays.
Bait imitated: Generic attractor (squid variation has black spots).

TROPICAL PUNCH (created by Dan Blanton)

Hook: Size 2/0 (sample: TMC 811S, Eagle Claw 254 CAT).
Thread: Hot orange Nymo "A" or equivalent.
Eyes: Large silver bead chain.
Tail: Yellow bucktail.
Tail Flash: Gold Flashabou, 25 to 30 strands of per side.
Body: Gold Mylar, wrapped.
Hackle: Yellow saddle hackle, large and webbed.
Topping: Layered yellow Krystal Hair, peacock Krystal Hair, then 10 to 15 strands of peacock herl.
Wing: Hot orange grizzly saddle hackle, 1 per side.
Head: Hot orange medium chenille, topped with peacock herl.
Target species: Rockfish, calico bass.
Habitat use: Rocky shores, kelp beds, harbors.
Bait imitated: Generic attractor.

V-WORM (created by Andy Burk)

Hook: Size 10 to 6 (TMC 8089NP).
Weed guard: Hard Mason monofilament (optional).
Thread: Match body color, 6/0 standard or 3/0 monocord.
Tail: Five inches of Vernille or Ultra Chenille (color variations include black, olive, rusty brown, or purple).
Tip: Fluorescent green or orange marabou.
Body: Buggy Nymph dubbing to match tail color. Use permanent markers for accent stripes or spots.
Target species: Flatfish, striped bass, sand bass.
Habitat use: Estuaries.
Bait imitated: Various marine worms.

Bibliography

America's Seashore Wonderlands. Washington, D.C.: National Geographic Society, Special Publications Division, 1985.

Bond, Carl E., and Alan J. Beardsley. *Field Guide to Common Marine and Bay Fishes of Oregon.* Corvallis: Oregon State University Agriculture Experiment Station, Extension Manual 4, 1984.

Carefoot, Thomas. *Pacific Seashores: A Guide to Intertidal Ecology.* Seattle: University of Washington Press, 1977.
Carson, Rachel. *The Edge of the Sea.* Boston: Houghton Mifflin, 1979.

Clemens, W. A., and G. V. Wilby. *Fishes of the Pacific Coast of Canada.* 2d ed. Ottowa: Bulletin of the Fisheries Research Board of Canada 68, 1961.

Dawson, E. Yale. *Marine Botany: An Introduction.* New York: Holt, Rinehart & Winston, 1966.

———— and Michael S. Foster. *Seashore Plants of California.* Berkeley: University of California Press, 1982.

Eschmeyer, William N., Earl S. Herald, Howard Hammann, and Kathryn P. Smith. *Pacific Coast Fishes of North America.* Boston: Houghton Mifflin, 1984.

Gotshell, Daniel W. *Pacific Coast Inshore Fishes.* Los Osos, California: Sea Challengers, Western Marine Enterprises, 1981.

Hitz, Charles R. *Field Indentification of the Northeastern Pacific Rockfish.* Washington, D.C.: U.S. Fish and Wildlife Service Circular 203, 1977.

Kelley, Don Greame. *Edge of a Continent: The Pacific Coast from Alaska to Baja.* Palo Alto, California: American West Publishing, 1971.

McConnaughey, Bayard H., and Evelyn McConnaughey. *Pacific Coast.* 5th ed. New York: Alfred A. Knopf, 1990.

McLusky, D. S. *Ecology of Estuaries.* London: Heinemann Educational Books, 1971.

Miller, Daniel J., and Robert N. Lea. *Guide to the Coastal Marine Fishes of California.* California Department of Fish and Game, Fish Bulletin 157, 1972.

Natural History of the Monterey Bay National Marine Sanctuary. Monterey, California: Monterey Bay Aquarium Foundation, 1997.

Niesen, Thomas M. *Beachcomber's Guide to Marine Life of the Pacific Northwest.* Houston, Texas: Gulf Publishing Company, 1997.

O'Clair, Charles E., and Rita M. O'Clair. *Southeast Alaska's Rocky Shores, Animals.* Auke Bay, Alaska: Plant Press, 1998.

Ricketts, Edward F., Jack Calvin, and Joel W. Hedspeth. Revised by David W. Phillips. *Between Pacific Tides.* 5th ed. Stanford, California: Stanford University Press, 1968.

Sumich, James L. *An Introduction to the Biology of Marine Life.* 4th ed. Dubuque, Iowa: Wm. C. Brown Company, 1968.

Tidelog. Available in the following editions covering the Pacific coastal region: Puget Sound (the entire Puget Sound region and part of the San Juan Islands), Northern California (from Monterey, California north to the Nehalem River, Oregon), and Southern California (from Carmel, California down through Mexico). Contact Pacific Publishers, Box 480, Bolinas CA 94924.

Index